# We're Talking Millions!

## 12 Ways to Supercharge Your Retirement

## Paul Merriman and Richard Buck

The Merriman
Financial Education
Foundation

# We're Talking Millions!
## 12 Ways to Supercharge Your Retirement
© 2020 by Paul Merriman and Richard Buck

ISBN: 978-1-7361196-0-0

Editorial Consultant – Aysha Griffin
Formatting Maven — Margie Baxley
Cover Designer — Anahi Aliaga
Cover Conceptualizer — Tree Elven
Proofreader – Thomas Haney

*We're Talking Millions!*

# ALSO BY PAUL MERRIMAN and RICHARD BUCK

### *How To Invest Series*:

*Free downloads available at* paulmerriman.com

**First Time Investor:** Grow and Protect Your Money

**Get Smart or Get Screwed:** How To Select The Best and Get The Most From Your Financial Advisor

**101 Investment Decisions** Guaranteed To Change Your Financial Future

**Financial Fitness Forever** — 5 Steps To More Money, Less Risk, More Peace of Mind

**Live It Up Without Outliving Your Money:** Creating The Perfect Retirement

Paul Merriman and Richard Buck

To all those seeking a simple blueprint
for a favorable financial future.

▲

# Praise for We're Talking Millions!

Paul and Richard reduce the complexity of saving for retirement into strategies anyone can follow. Regardless if you are new to investing or have been investing for years, you'll find suggestions for boosting your wealth with minimal effort required.

> — Charles Rotblut, CFA, *AAII Journal* Editor and VP American Association of Individual Investors

Whether millennial or boomer, understanding these 12 concepts can have a big financial payoff... *We're Talking Millions!* Paul Merriman and Richard Buck team up again to educate and motivate."

> — David Baughier, curator of Fiology.com

Merriman and Buck have done a great job of giving a playbook for financial success that anyone can read and understand!"

> — George Grombacher, host of the "Money Savage" podcast

Paul & Rich have done it again! For the last few decades they have shown investors how to create long-term portfolios for retirement, how to generate retirement income, and how to avoid costly mistakes. In their new book, *We're Talking Millions! 12 Ways to Supercharge Your Retirement*, they help people of all ages with huge money decisions. Written in plain English with critical charts, this book will help anyone who wants to create wealth in simple, low cost ways.

> — Tom Cock, co-host "Talking Real Money"

*We're Talking Millions*! could be a young person's Most Valuable Read (MVR) of their life, if they take action!
— Ed Fulbright, CPA,PFS, host of Masteringyourmoney.com

I have always said that investing is too easy to seem so complex. Paul Merriman and Rich Buck have managed to prove that point in this powerful and easily understood guide to building wealth. Their approach is so straightforward and simple that anyone can build a sensible, science-based portfolio almost immediately. Follow this advice and you could be "talking millions" in your pocket.
— Don McDonald, co-host "Talking Real Money", author *Financial Fysics*

*This book is a must-read for anybody wanting to take control of their finances and build wealth the smart way. Paul and Richard take sophisticated concepts and boil them down into easy to understand and follow steps. I just wish they had written the book 30 years ago!*
— Rob Berger, author of *Retire Before Mom and Dad*

*We're Talking Millions!*

# TABLE OF CONTENTS

# FOREWARD
by Richard Buck

When Paul Merriman first told me he wanted me to work with him in writing this book, I said no thanks. I was happily retired, and I feared that we would end up repeating ideas about which we had already written.

My reticence didn't have anything to do with Paul.

He and I have worked together since 1993. We have written six previous books as well as countless articles and newsletters. We're good friends, we work well together, and we're often able to anticipate the other's thoughts and objections and preferences. We laugh together, and our wives know that when we get on the phone, the conversation may go on and on.

Fortunately, Paul persisted with the idea for this book.

For many years I've been a fan of his Ultimate Buy and Hold Strategy for long-term investors. It's the basis for how most of my own money is invested.

At the same time, I've been reluctant to recommend that strategy to people I know because it's complex to put into practice.

So when Paul told me he had found a way to capture nearly all the benefits of the Ultimate Buy and Hold Strategy using only two readily available mutual funds, I was very interested, though skeptical.

When he told me exactly what he had in mind and showed me some of the data to support it, I immediately saw the value. Fortunately, I said yes to this project.

While Paul and I were working on this book, I was delighted to find its message easy to explain and describe to friends and family members. That certainly seemed like a good sign.

Over the course of writing this book, Paul and I have wrestled with numerous issues, including:

- How much data and detail will our target audience of young readers tolerate?
- How much do they really have to know?
- How do we keep the specific recommendations simple enough that anyone can carry them out, while still accommodating all the variables?

Paul is a guy who likes to teach using numbers, tables, and charts. Lots of them. I prefer to teach using stories, perhaps reflecting my 30 years as a journalist.

As it turns out, we found a way to accurately describe this strategy without resorting to large tables of numbers. You'll find small tables in some chapters, but each one had to pass two tests: (1) does it point to something essential? and (2) is a table the best way to make the point?

We have done our best to strike a balance, keeping the message understandable and simple to implement while giving you, the reader, enough information to have confidence in our recommendations. You, of course, will be the ultimate judge of how well we succeeded.

Writing a book with two authors can be awkward. Each of us has lots of experience that we want to share personally. You deserve to know when something comes specifically from Paul and when something comes specifically from me. How do we do that gracefully when pronouns such as "I" and "mine" don't really work with two authors?

Our answer finally emerged when Paul and I realized that almost everything in this book actually comes from both of us, reflecting our agreement and rough-and-tumble discussions about all of the material.

In the pages that follow, you will occasionally see material in italics that's clearly labeled as coming from one or the other of us.

Everything else represents our combined thinking, and there is nothing about which we disagree.

I hope you'll read our Introduction. Like most of the chapters in this book, I think it would satisfy the way my father used to describe a speech or presentation that he liked: "Mercifully brief!"

# INTRODUCTION

## WHY WE WROTE THIS BOOK

This book is designed to show you how you can change your life by making a handful of smart choices. It's a recipe for potentially accumulating millions of dollars you can spend in retirement and leave to your heirs.

There's no magic here, just common sense.

If you want a complete understanding of risk, investment theory, asset classes, or mutual fund analysis, this book won't give you that.

Our job in these pages is to provide simple explanations of the most important things every investor should do—and to give you relatively simple instructions on how to do them.

Your job is not to be a financial wizard or a lucky lottery winner. Your job is to be a normal person who can and will regularly set aside a small part of your income and stick to a simple plan for the years before you retire.

*Paul: Ever since the 1960s when, for a few years, I was a fresh-out-of-college broker on Wall Street, I've focused the majority of my time and energy on helping real people get the most benefit from their investments.*

*Although I've spent a lot of time helping people with substantial amounts of money, I've always been concerned that not enough young people—perhaps like you—are on track to accumulate the money they will need to retire comfortably.*

*That concern is what's behind this book.*

The heart of this book is 12 Small Steps with Big Payoffs. Each one of these steps can potentially add $1 million to the retirement nest egg of somebody who applies it starting in their 20s or early 30s. These steps are well-known to savvy investors and advisors.

But one thing is new: an action plan that applies them in a single solution that can be carried out easily by just about anybody who has a job.

We call this plan Two Funds for Life. It's designed to make a big difference in the amount of money you'll have to spend during retirement and eventually leave to your heirs. Exactly how big that difference will be is impossible to say because there are so many variables.

But we believe it's reasonable to think this strategy could easily double the dollars you have when you retire. The difference could be much greater, especially if you implement this strategy in your 20s.

You might benefit from knowing the origin of the Two Funds for Life strategy. So here's the short history.

## The very best way to invest for the long term

*Paul: In the 1990s, I found a way to assemble some of the most powerful financial building blocks I'm aware of and organize them into an investment portfolio that I called The Ultimate Buy and Hold Strategy. There is nothing casual about my choice of the word "ultimate." It's the very best that I know. Period.*

The two of us have worked together since then to make this strategy available to investors.

Based on the best academic research available, we believe that strategy is the absolute best way for most investors to achieve long-term growth in the stock markets. This strategy is the basis of most of our own investments.

In a nutshell, this "ultimate" portfolio starts with the Standard & Poor's (S&P) 500 Index, a stock market index that tracks the stocks of 500 large U.S. companies. It then adds equal portions of nine other pools of carefully chosen types of U.S. and international stocks. (Stocks are also called equities and signify ownership in a company.) Each "pool" is an asset class made up of stocks with similar characteristics. This portfolio has been an excellent long-term diversification vehicle.

(Diversification is a defensive investment strategy that can be neatly summed up as "Don't put all your eggs in one basket." In this book, diversification refers mostly to the practice of owning more than one asset class.)

The result is a low-coststock portfolio with massive diversification that will take advantage of market opportunities wherever they are, with about the same risk as that of the S&P 500 Index.

There's just one problem with this terrific strategy, and it's a big one: Putting it to work is neither easy nor convenient.

## Here's where Two Funds for Life enters the picture

There is no way to achieve this Ultimate Buy and Hold Strategy portfolio with only one or two funds. It takes ten, plus an 11th for investors who want or need a bond fund to reduce risk, and that should include most people. (A bond fund invests primarily in bonds and similar securities.)

*Paul: Some years ago, I investigated what it would take to create a single mutual fund to capture all these asset classes, but the costs and complexity were much too great.*

*Fast forward to 2017, when I met a fellow retiree who is very good with numbers and research and shares my strong desire to help investors. His name is Chris Pedersen, and he accepted a challenge that seemed pretty tough: Find a way to provide most of the benefits of the Ultimate Buy and Hold Strategy using only two mutual funds.*

*(Mutual funds are a form of collective investment in which money from many investors is pooled and invested in stocks, bonds, short-term money market instruments, or other securities under the direction of a fund manager.)*

*I wanted a solution that would take care of investors throughout their lives, with very little attention needed from them.*

*After much discussion of many potential variations, Two Funds for Life emerged from that challenge.*

Young investors today have access to some terrific tools that didn't exist when we started investing in the mid-20th century. Information and historical data that once seemed the exclusive domain of Wall Street insiders and their wealthy clients are now readily available to anyone who knows where to look for it.

This book references some of that information. More important, it shows how to put those tools and that information to work for you.

We believe that investors of all ages can benefit from the approach outlined here. While the greatest benefits will accrue to young investors who have lots of time to let their money grow, it's never too late to give your retirement savings a boost using the information and suggestions in this book.

Even starting at age 65, applying these lessons could potentially be worth an extra $1 million.

## Economic pain and uncertainty

As we complete this book, unemployment and economic pain are higher than they've been for decades, and the world is facing a huge health and economic crisis that seems as if it could continue for some time.

Jobs have disappeared, government financial support is floundering, and many industries are imploding. Teachers, students, restaurant owners, renters, landlords, travel agents, health care providers, entertainers—all these and many more are staring into a future that can feel discouraging at best and depressing at worst.

In the summer of 2020, Federal Reserve Chairman Jerome Powell said that our economic future is "extraordinarily uncertain" right now.

The bad news is obvious, and it affects everybody. Many investors and potential investors may be thinking along the lines of "this is just terrible."

Later in this book, we strongly advise against timing the market based on emotions.

When millions of people ask how things could get any worse, that's often as close as you will ever get to a "buy" signal.

The good news is that at some point, things will clear up a bit and people will feel more confident about the future. This is where successful investing starts. As uncomfortable as it seems, based on our experience over more than 50 years, this smells like opportunity.
Even if you can save only $100, we hope you will find a way to do that and do it sooner than later. When the clouds that hover over us dissipate, the stock market is likely to reward those who had enough long-term faith to be invested.

It's never too late to start. It's never too early to start. And there's no shame in starting small.

## What we want from you, our reader

Our goal is to get you to take action. If we don't persuade you to do something, then we've missed the mark.

What we recommend won't take long to implement. We once calculated that it takes roughly 16,000 hours to get through high school and earn a bachelor's degree. Experts say it takes at least 2,000 hours to master a skill such as playing an instrument or learning to fly.

If you're enrolled in a 401(k) or similar retirement plan at work, you can implement our recommendations in about an hour—two hours at the most. That could be the most valuable time you'll ever spend.

That hour or two, plus maybe 30 minutes or so a year thereafter, could be worth millions of dollars over your lifetime.

## Terminology

This work contains some terminology that is familiar to many investors but can sound like insider jargon to lots of people who could benefit from this work. Accordingly, you will find a small glossary in the back of the book of terms and phrases that should help you follow along. We also have made a point to explain concepts as we go.

*We're Talking Millions!*

We've tried to keep this book relatively short, giving you enough background to know why we recommend each step, without burying you in unnecessary details.

So whenever you're ready, let's roll up our sleeves and begin.

*Paul Merriman and Richard Buck, August 2020*

Paul Merriman and Richard Buck

# Section One

# SMALL STEPS WITH BIG PAYOFFS

▲

Paul Merriman and Richard Buck

# INTRODUCTION TO SECTION ONE

## The elephant in the room: Inflation

In this book, we toss around a lot of pretty big numbers. Add $1 million to your retirement. Retire with $1,932,520 at age 65 (cited in Chapter 2).

Numbers like that may seem like a fantasy that's just too unrealistic to take seriously.

Many young people today might be happy to contemplate someday having investments worth even $500,000, let alone millions.

We get it.

There's an old saying that "numbers don't lie." But that's not always true.

Some of the numbers in this book may seem preposterous. They aren't. You just have to understand them, and that means taking long-term inflation into consideration. (Inflation is a gradual increase in prices along with a decline in the purchasing power of money.)

For example, in the pages that follow, you will read projections of 40-year investment returns that result in very big numbers. But the reality of having $1 million 40 years from now might fall short of your fantasies.

Forty years of actual inflation from 1980 to 2020 reduced the purchasing power of $1,000 to slightly less than $300. So when you think about a figure 40 years in the future, if you divide by three you may be somewhere in the ballpark of understanding it.

When you're planning for a very long timeframe at 3% inflation, $1 million today will be worth about $228,000 in 50 years.

That may be the bad news. The good news is that if you follow the recommendations in this book, your money is likely to grow significantly faster than inflation erodes it.

If you achieve a compound return of 10%, which is historically realistic for stock investments, and inflation is 3% (also realistic historically), your investments should grow by 7% in actual value.

In that scenario, a one-time investment of $100 becomes worth $197 after 10 years; in other words, it buys about twice what it did when you socked it away.

Here's what happens to that $100 over longer periods:

- After 20 years, it's really worth about $387
- After 30 years, really worth about $761
- After 40 years, really worth about $1,497

Based on 10% investment returns and 3% inflation, those numbers are real.

We haven't tried to adjust the figures in this book to account for inflation. But here are two things you should keep in mind:

- First, the really big numbers aren't as preposterous as they might seem.
- Second, long-term favorable investment returns can greatly increase the purchasing power of every dollar you save.

No matter what your age or how much money you save, that is really worth doing.

## Small Steps with Big Payoffs

In this section, we outline a dozen decisions, each one of which is potentially worth at least $1 million over your lifetime of working, saving, and investing.

Of course, $1 million won't materialize out of thin air. You will have to save money, invest it wisely, and give it time.

Furthermore, we're not promising that these 12 steps will add up cumulatively to $12 million. But if you make these decisions properly and then act on them, you may someday be counting your money in million-dollar increments.

We call these 12 Small Steps with Big Payoffs.

Your life is your own to plan, manage, and carry out as you see fit.

We've narrowed the variables into a dozen important decisions that you will make—whether or not you realize you are making them.

These decisions aren't necessarily easy, and you might have noticed that the world isn't populated with billions of millionaires. But each one of these steps is simple to understand and execute. Each one is (mostly) in your control. Each one, all by itself, can have huge implications for your lifetime financial situation.

Obviously, there are many other variables in your life in addition to these 12. Luck (good or bad), mistakes, and unexpected events all play a big part in determining how our lives play out.

## What you can count on

We can tell you three things for sure:

1. If you make these 12 choices correctly and do your best to carry them out, you won't really need the material in the latter parts of the book.

2. If you fail to make these choices properly, the material in the rest of the book won't be of much help.

3.  If you make these 12 choices correctly *and* apply what's in the rest of the book, you will be among the most successful investors of your generation.

Here are these 12 Small Steps with Big Payoffs:

1.  Save some money instead of spending it all.

2.  Start saving sooner instead of later.

3.  Invest your savings in stocks instead of bonds and cash.

4.  Invest in many stocks instead of only a few.

5.  Keep your expenses low.

6.  Choose index funds instead of actively managed funds.

7.  Include small-company stocks in your portfolio.

8.  Include value stocks in your portfolio.

9.  Don't try to "time" the market or outwit it.

10. Invest using dollar-cost averaging instead of waiting for the right time to invest.

11. Keep your taxes low.

12. Do all this in one simple step: Invest in a target date retirement fund.

Some of the chapters describing these steps are quite short. Others are a bit longer. In each case, we've tried to make the most important points without unnecessarily belaboring them.

That's the overview. Now let's dig in.

Paul Merriman and Richard Buck

1.

# Small Step #1:

# **Save Instead of Spend**

*"Do not save what is left after spending; instead spend what is left after saving."*
Warren Buffett

Of all the Small Steps in this book, this is in a way the biggest. It's by far the most impactful in separating those who attain financial independence from those who don't.

Two things are immediately obvious. First, you can't save and invest some of your money if you spend it all. Second, you can't save *all* your money; you've got to have some to live (and enjoy) your life.

Based on the assumptions outlined in the introduction to this section, to get a $1 million payoff from this Small

22

Step, you'll need to accumulate $300,000 by the time you're 65. That's not nearly as daunting as it seems.

If your investments grow at 8% annually, that requires putting away about $62 a month starting when you're 21 (or $86 a month if you start at age 25, or $130 a month if you start when you're 30).

This Small Step (saving money) is simple, but in a world filled with constant messages that urge you to splurge, it isn't easy.

Young people have the best opportunities to let their savings compound for the long periods of time that can provide the Big Payoff. But many young people are saddled with significant student debt in addition to the costs of establishing households and families.

If you want to retire with adequate resources, you will have to find some way to save. There's no way around it.

## Get to first base

We could go on and on about this topic, but it doesn't require much elaboration. Either you are going to set aside money for your future, or you aren't.

To do this, you'll have to figure out and actually do whatever it takes to "live below your means" and spend less than you could.

We can't overemphasize this point: Unless you delay some of your gratification by saving instead of spending everything that you have, you won't even get to first base as an investor.

If you don't see a way forward, there are people who will be happy to help you, without cost or any conflict of interest.

There's an international movement of people who support each other in building their savings and investment assets rapidly so they can retire early. The movement is known as "FIRE," which stands for Financial Independence Retire Early. One of the best known organizations within this movement is called ChooseFI, with the "FI" standing for Financial Independence.

*Paul: I have spoken to some of their local chapters and met some of their key players. Without exception, they have told me they are willing to share what they have learned.*

*At an online site called Choosefi.com, you can learn more, perhaps find a chapter near you, join one of their Facebook groups, leave a voicemail, or send a written message online asking for help.*

The bottom line here: You *can* take this all-important step.

# 2.

# Small Step #2:

# **Start Saving Earlier Instead of Later**

*"You don't have to see the whole staircase to take the first step."*
Martin Luther King Jr.

The more thoroughly you apply this Small Step, the bigger your Big Payoff will be.

Here's a simple table to make the point.

**Table 2-1**: Results of investing sooner, assuming an 8% compound return.

| If you invest $100 at | At age 65, you'll have: |
|---|---|
| Age 20 | $3,192 |
| Age 25 | $2,172 |
| Age 30 | $1,478 |
| Age 35 | $1,006 |
| Age 40 | $684 |
| Age 45 | $466 |
| Age 50 | $317 |
| Age 55 | $215 |

Table 2-2 presents that same lesson from a slightly different point of view. It calculates how big your one-time investment would need to be, again assuming an 8% compound return, at various ages to accumulate $100,000 by the time you're 65.

**Table 2-2**: Increasing amounts needed to achieve $100,000 by age 65.

| If you invest once at | Amount needed to reach $100,000 at age 65 |
|---|---|
| Age 20 | $3,133 |
| Age 25 | $4,603 |
| Age 30 | $6,764 |
| Age 35 | $9,938 |
| Age 40 | $14,602 |
| Age 45 | $21,455 |
| Age 50 | $31,524 |
| Age 55 | $46,319 |

As the table shows, you *can* achieve a goal even if you wait a long time before you start. But the longer you wait, the harder it gets. And the curve is steep.

In the previous chapter, we said you would need to accumulate $300,000 by age 65 in order to have a $1 million lifetime payoff. The top line of Table 2-2 shows you could do that with a one-time investment at age 20 of less than $10,000 ($9,399, to be exact).

Obviously, most 20-year-olds don't have an extra $9,399 just waiting to be put to work. But consider the following:

This is getting ahead a bit, but the figure $9,399 assumes an annualized return of 8%. In this book, we'll show you how, based on over 90 years of historical returns, you may get 10% or even 12%. At 12%, you could start with about $1,830 at age 20 and reach that $300,000 mark by the time you're 65.

That lifetime $1 million might be easier to achieve than you think.

Not to belabor the point too much, but there's one more very interesting way to show the value of early savings.

## The first 10 years

Imagine you're saving a constant $5,000 a year from age 21 to 65, a total of 45 years. That means that every 10 years, you add $50,000 to your investments.

Assuming a steady 8% compound return, the ultimate value of your first 10 years of savings will be much greater than the value of the $50,000 you add in any subsequent 10-year period:

- Your first $50,000 (the money you save from age 21 through 30) grows to 1,070,940 by your 65th birthday.
- Your second $50,000 (your savings in your 30s) grows to $496,050.

- Your third $50,000 (your savings in your 40s) grows to $229,769.
- Your fourth $50,000 (your savings in your 50s) grows to $106,428.
- Finally, your last five years of savings ($25,000) before age 65 grows to only $29,333.

In this scenario, you wind up with $1,932,520 at age 65. The majority of it, 55.4%, came from that first decade of savings. For every $1 you saved in that period, you wind up with about $21.40.

Contrast that with this calculation: Only about one-quarter of your retirement nest egg came from the $50,000 you saved in your 30s.

This scenario, of course, assumes constant returns of 8% every year. Everything we know about the past tells us that the future won't be that neat and predictable. Returns will be high some years and low in other years. Some years will be positive, some negative.

But regardless of the returns you get, the advantage of saving earlier is huge.

Is this decision worth $1 million? Here's why we think so: If you started investing $5,000 a year at age 31 instead of 21, your nest egg at retirement would be only $861,580 instead of $1.93 million. That is a difference of over $1 million.

So put time on your side, even if you have to start small. You won't be sorry.

## A semi-radical idea

*Paul: Starting early makes such a huge difference that some of my friends who understand this have actually loaned money to their own kids to help them start investing earlier.*

*In one case I know, this meant a young woman could afford to contribute to her company's retirement plan and get the benefit of a company match. In a couple of other cases, young people used the proceeds of a parental loan to contribute to a Roth IRA that started growing tax-free.*

*I made gifts like this to my own kids when they were young. I told them that if they used the money for anything other than investing, that was the last money they would ever get from me (as far as I know, this threat has worked!).*

You'll have to decide whether you feel comfortable proposing such an arrangement with your own parents.

But if you do, you should totally respect their financial needs. Maybe you start by showing them some of what you have learned in this chapter.

Then make a proposal that you think will be mutually beneficial. If they have financial assets that are earning relatively low interest rates, you could propose to pay them a higher rate in return for a long-term loan.

It's easy to get bogged down in details, but here's one possibility: You ask for a one-time loan to fund a Roth IRA and promise you'll pay it back, with accrued interest, in 10 years (when presumably you'll have the income to afford doing that).

If you repeated that arrangement every year until that first payment was due (10 years, in other words), your retirement savings would get an enormous head start. And your parents could look forward to 10 years of payments from you.

Here's another possibility: If your folks seem to have ample assets, you could propose that they give you an "advance" on your inheritance, on which you would pay interest only. Presumably, that interest might come back to you someday in the form of an inheritance.

Your pitch to them: The money that you hope to inherit someday will be vastly more valuable to you now than it would be 40 or 50 years down the road. Maybe they'll go for it; maybe they won't.

But if nothing else, by showing them that you're studying this book, you'll be demonstrating financial responsibility and foresight. Most parents would be happy to see such a demonstration.

(Just make sure you don't come off as pleading with them for money!)

# 3.

## Small Step #3

# Invest in Stocks, Not Bonds

*"An important key to investing is to remember that stocks are not lottery tickets."*
Peter Lynch, manager (1977–1990) of Fidelity Magellan,
the number one growth fund at the time,
which compounded at 29% on his watch.

The basic divide in the investment world is between stocks (we will sometimes refer to them as equities, and throughout this book we'll use those two terms interchangeably) and bonds.

Here is the basic difference between equities and bonds:

- **Equities** represent ownership. When you buy stock in a company, you own part of it. As a stockholder, you get part of the benefits if everything goes right. At the same time, you assume some of the risk that the business could flop. Your payback takes two forms: First, you can sell your stock to another investor; second, you can receive dividends, which are distributions that some companies pay to shareholders.

- **Bonds** represent loans. When you buy a bond from a company or a government entity, you are lending money. You own a promise that the money will be repaid, with interest, over an agreed-upon time. Your payback doesn't depend on whether the company does well or does poorly. If you're a bondholder, your risk is lower, and the money that's due to you will be repaid before the shareholders get a dime. As a lender, you incur the risk that the borrower could default, partially or completely.

"Given the choice between stocks and bonds," said Warren Buffet, "I would choose equities in a minute."

## Risk vs. return

Here's the most important thing about this: Stocks have a long history of being more profitable than bonds. But stocks are also riskier than bonds.

What follows is an oversimplification of a complex and important topic (but we're seeking million-dollar decisions, so let's look at the big picture).

If you're in your 20s, 30s, 40s, 50s, or even your 60s, owning stocks instead of bonds is potentially a million-dollar decision. The more years you have before you, the bigger the difference.

We don't want to bury you with numbers, but here are a few you should know.

## Double your money

From 1928 through 2019, the average compound 40-year return of long-term U.S. government bonds was 5.5%. At that rate, you can expect to double your money about every 13.1 years.

Over the same time frame, the average compound 40-year return of the U.S. stock market (defined for our purposes as the Standard & Poor's 500 Index) was 10.9%. At that rate, you can expect to double your money about every seven years (this assumes you reinvested any dividends you received instead of taking that money in cash).

That's a bigger difference than it seems. Over 40 years, stocks would double almost six times, and bonds three times.

For an investor adding $5,000 a year for 40 years, the historical 5.5% return of bonds would result in $683,028; the 10.9% return of the S&P 500 would result in $2.83 million.

Need we say more? Well, yes.

Most investors are unlikely to be either 100% in stocks or 100% bonds for 40 years. A long-term return of 8% is reasonable for a combination of stocks and bonds that gradually moves away from stocks as the investor approaches retirement. An 8% return over 40 years (assuming additional savings of $5,000 a year) would be worth about $1.3 million, roughly twice the return of an all-bond portfolio.

Just about any way you look at it, using stocks for most or all of your portfolio is likely to lead to an advantage of $1 million or more.

## Why bonds?

So why do investors like bonds? In a word, safety.

*Paul: I'm 77, and roughly half my investments are in bond funds. This allocation reduces the impact of the ups and downs of the stock market on my portfolio and gives me peace of mind.*

*Richard: I'm roughly the same age, and bonds make up around 30% of my own investments.*

But if you are in your early years of saving and investing, it would be a huge mistake to use bonds for a major part of your portfolio. What young people need is growth, not "protection" from temporary stock market fluctuations.

However, stocks, also called equities, should be chosen well. That's our topic in Chapter 4.

4.

## Small Step #4

# Own Many Stocks Instead of Only a Few

*"Don't look for the needle in the haystack.*
*Just buy the haystack!"*
John C. Bogle, founder of The Vanguard Group

One of the biggest mistakes that investors make— especially young investors— is trying to win big in the stock market. It's easy to see the huge profits some people have made by owning a few dazzling stocks like Apple, Microsoft, Amazon, and Google, or for a previous generation, General Electric, Johnson & Johnson, International Business Machines, and so on.

But, you ask, with all the information now available, how hard can it be to find the next winner and ride the market to riches? Mighty hard, as it turns out.

It's theoretically possible to get lucky. People who invested $10,000 in Microsoft in 1986 and hung on were worth about $3 million at the end of 1999. Easy money, right?

But if you were late to the party and didn't buy Microsoft stock until 1999, you unknowingly opened yourself up to a world of hurt. After just a few months you would have lost more than half your investment.

If you were extremely patient (some people would say stubborn) and kept that Microsoft stock, you would have finally broken even—16 years later!

## More is more

No matter how much you may want to try your hand at picking future stock market winners, a much better idea is to buy many stocks. That way, if any of them gets into trouble and goes into a tailspin, you still have all the others. This is called diversification, and it's one of the most important lessons investors should learn.

Still, more is more, and in this case, it's also better.

In the old days, most lists of "best stocks to own" came out at the end of a calendar year and purported to predict the best performers of the upcoming year. Then in 1972, lists started appearing of stocks to own and keep forever. The most popular ones were called the "Nifty 50," and the premise was that these companies were so terrific that you'd never have any reason to dump them for others.

However, "forever" didn't last as long as many of those hopeful investors thought it would.

Investors who bought the 50 "best" stocks back then and held onto them have made considerably less money than the Standard & Poor's 500 Index, a common proxy for the U.S. stock market as a whole.

Over the long haul, owning 50 stocks is definitely better than owning just a few. Owning 500 is definitely more advantageous than owning 50. And as we'll discuss shortly, owning thousands of stocks is hands-down better than owning "only" 500.

Over the past 90 years, the U.S. stock market has grown around 10% per year, though of course not in a straight line. A landmark academic study that came out a few years ago reached a startling conclusion: This 10% return could be traced to fewer than 4% of all public companies.

On average, the stocks of the other 96% returned about 3% a year, similar to the return of Treasury bills. If that pattern continues—and we have no reason to think it won't—then your chances of finding a blockbuster stock are about one in 25.

That's the bad news. The good news is that if you owned **all** the stocks, you would have received that 10% return.

It seems counter-intuitive, but additional academic studies indicate that investing in more stocks leads to higher returns, not lower returns.

So, is this really a million-dollar decision?

We say yes, because we are dealing with probabilities. It's *possible* you'll identify and invest in the next IBM or the next Apple. But it's not *probable*.

## A bonus point that's worth $1 million or more

There's another million-dollar piece of information lurking here, and because you've waded this far into this chapter, we'll give it to you now, at no extra charge.

Getting back to our narrative about owning many stocks instead of only a few, let's suppose that your compound return from owning many stocks is a mere half percentage point a year more than if you owned just a few. The difference is likely to be greater, but 0.5% will let us make our point.

Now assume you invest $5,000 a year from age 21 to age 65 in just a few stocks, and you earn 8% compounded annually. Then you scale back your portfolio so it earns 6% for the next 30 years. You'll presumably be withdrawing 4% of your portfolio every year during that time.

(Four percent is generally accepted as an annual withdrawal rate from your investments that's likely to survive whatever happens in the markets and to grow over time to at least keep up with inflation.)

At these rates of return, 8% and 6%, you'll have $1.4 million by the time you're 65, and after 30 years of retirement withdrawals, your end-of-life portfolio will be worth about $2.4 million—and that's in addition to $2.2 million you will have taken during your retirement. That total of about $4.6 million is not bad at all for investing $200,000 of your own money. But it can be better.

As an alternative, let's assume you take the advice of this chapter to heart. You diversify your portfolio by owning hundreds of stocks instead of only a few; assume this gives you a compound return of 8.5% until you're 65, and 6.5% after that.

At age 65, you'll retire with about $1.6 million, and after 30 years of retirement withdrawals, your portfolio will be worth $3.1 million, in addition to retirement withdrawals of $2.7 million over 30 years—a total of about $5.8 million.

That's an extra $1.2 million for you to live on and leave to your fortunate heirs, and that extra came from a mere

0.5% increase in your rate of return. And capturing that extra 0.5% is easy, as we're about to see.

That's how a very Small Step can turn into a very Big Payoff.

## Owning many stocks is easy

Fortunately, owning hundreds of stocks is as easy as owning only a few. You can do this by owning index funds, which we discuss in Chapter 6. This will give you professional management, broad diversification, and easy record-keeping, all for very little cost.

For many investors, the notion that returns are higher from owning more companies than from only a few is a hard pill to swallow. It goes against the notion that hard work and diligent study will be rewarded.

Putting your money in a single company is considered speculation, while owning hundreds of companies is considered an investment. Why? The single company carries the huge risk that it could hit not only hard times but go out of business or be acquired in a way that is not in the best interests of stockholders.

This is called business risk, and it's virtually non-existent in a portfolio made up of hundreds of companies.

Even if you find it hard to get your head around the concept, take our word for it: You'll almost certainly do better if you own many companies than if you own only a few.

# 5.

# Small Step #5

# Cut Your Investment Expenses

*"The two greatest enemies of the equity fund investor are expenses and emotions."*
John C. Bogle

Want a really easy way to get higher returns? This is it.

No matter what you invest in (and even if you ignore all the other advice in this book), every dollar you save in investment expenses is a dollar that's added to your return.

You won't be able to eliminate fees and expenses entirely. It costs money to keep your account records accurate, safe, and up to date. It costs money to administer your investments, and you want all that to be done properly. For that, you will need to pay something.

However, unnecessary expenses and fees are your enemy.

## A leaky bucket

Imagine your portfolio as a bucket gradually filling up with water. The water inside represents your wealth. Now picture a tiny rupture in the bottom of the bucket through which a little bit of water seeps out. That could describe the investment expenses you pay.

Your job in this step is to keep that drip-drip-drip to a minimum.

In the previous chapter, we saw that a difference of 0.5% per year in return, when applied to a lifetime of investing, could add up to about $1.2 million.

Trimming just 0.5% a year from your expenses would have a similar outcome, and it's easy to do. But lots of investors fail to take this step, and they pay through the nose.

Consider two very popular actively managed U.S. mutual funds.

Investors have parked $111.5 billion in Fidelity's Contrafund, which charges annual expenses of 0.85%, and $188.3 billion in American Funds' The Growth Fund of America, which charges 0.65%.

Collectively, that means investors are paying nearly $172 million every year in just these two funds.

Each of those funds is designed to outperform the Russell 1000 Growth Index, which is available in the iShares Russell 1000 Growth exchange-traded fund with expenses of just 0.19%.

But wait: The mutual funds' active management should provide higher returns to justify their higher expenses, right?

As it turns out, exactly the opposite is true. Over the past 10 years, as we write this in the summer of 2020, Fidelity Contrafund has underperformed its benchmark index by 1.5% a year, and Growth Fund of America has underperformed that benchmark index by 2.6% a year.

If all those investors had put their money in the exchange-traded fund we mentioned above, they would be saving about $1.7 billion a year. That money would be working for the investors instead of working for those fund companies.

(This lesson isn't just about expenses. It's also about actively managed funds vs. index funds—the topic of Chapter 6.)

Aside from choosing funds with low recurring expenses, there are some other ways you can cut your costs.

- Don't buy load funds, i.e., ones that pay a commission to a salesperson who signs you up.
- Avoid high-cost, high-commission products like variable annuities.
- Pay attention to taxes (Small Step 11).
- Beware of funds that engage in frequent trading, which incurs costs that can be cleverly hidden from your view.

If you use these principles to guide your investments and your behavior, you should have little trouble reducing your expenses by more than 0.5%, and thus raising your returns by at least that much.

As we saw before, that's worth at least $1 million.

Another Small Step with a Big Payoff.

# 6.

# Small Step #6
# **Choose Index Funds**

*"Index funds have regularly produced rates of
return exceeding those of active managers
by close to two percentage points."*
Burton Malkiel, author of *A Random Walk Down Wall Street*

Index funds deserve a place among your very best
friends.

An index fund is designed to replicate the performance
of an index such as the Standard & Poor's 500. Some
index funds own stocks, some own bonds, and some
own other types of securities. But each one is designed
to capture the performance of a specific group of
securities at a low cost.

By contrast, an actively managed fund typically owns fewer stocks, anywhere from a few dozen to 100. Its goal is to exceed the return of some particular index or benchmark. An active manager picks individual stocks, hoping to find those that will outperform the rest.

# If you can't beat it, join it

In an index fund, the management isn't trying to beat an index, only to reflect it.

Index funds have lower expenses, even down to zero. On average, according to some studies, actively managed funds charge 1% higher expenses than their respective index funds. That is *twice* the threshold for making this a $1 million decision.

These higher-than-necessary expenses deprive investors of a significant part of the returns they deserve for taking the risks of investing—and the additional risks of active management itself.

Index funds benefit investors in other ways: They have more diversification, which means less risk.

They are usually more tax efficient since they don't trade in hopes of beating the market.

Their lower trading volume shaves the costs of trading that are not included in expense ratios.

Index funds are available to track many types of stocks, including growth- and value-oriented flavors of large company stocks, small-company stocks, international stocks, emerging markets stocks, real estate investment trusts, and various types of bonds.

## A $1 million winner

Although specific results vary depending on the type of stock and the period under study, index funds outperform the vast majority of their actively managed competitors. For example, a 15-year study found that the S&P 500 Index funds did better than 92% of all U.S. large-company stock funds. For mid-cap funds, the figure was 95%; for small-company funds, it was nearly 94%.

Think about that: Over 15 years, only a tiny fraction of actively managed funds beat their benchmark.

To our way of thinking, an index fund that's likely to wind up in the top 10% of its peers—and does so while taking less risk and charging less money—is at least a $1 million winner.

7.

# Small Step #7

# **Invest in Small-Company Stocks**

*"You can measure opportunity with the same yardstick that measures the risk involved. They go together."*
Earl Nightingale, American author and motivational speaker

Once again, let's make sure we're on the same page and start with terminology. In the simplest terms, a small-company stock represents a company that's too small to be among the giants of the S&P 500 Index.

Every Microsoft, Apple, Google, and Facebook was once a small company. When their stocks were first issued, they were considered risky. What they all had in common was lots of room to grow. We're talking about growing A LOT.

Today, none of those companies would be even remotely in the ballpark of a small company. That doesn't mean they're bad investments. But it does mean they no longer have much potential to double, triple, and quadruple in size every few years.

Small-company stocks DO have that potential, though their names aren't normally household names.

Vanguard's Small Cap Index Fund owns nearly 1,400 stocks. You can be forgiven if you don't recognize these companies, which are among the fund's largest holdings: Exact Sciences, IDEX, Atmos Energy, Zebra Technologies, STERIS, and Leidos Holdings.

Investing in only a handful of small-company stocks is much too risky: A failure and implosion of only one company could wipe out a significant part of your portfolio. However, if you own these stocks by the hundreds, it takes only a few very successful ones to make up for many others that languish.

And if you own lots and lots of small-company stocks, you will get a piece of the action when that next long-shot idea explodes into success.

## A long profitable history

As a group, small-company stocks have a long history of success.

From 1928 through 2019, U.S. small-company stocks had a compound annual return of 12%, compared with 9.9% for the S&P 500. On a single $10,000 investment over a 40-year period, a return of 12% would grow to $930,510, compared with only $436,423 at 9.9%.

As we are about to see, such a difference is even more pronounced when we compare actual 40-year returns of small-company stocks with the S&P 500.

## 40 years

Forty years is a long time, but a reasonable period for a young person to evaluate investment returns. Heck, even somebody who's 55 may very well have a 40-year investing future.

With this in mind, we obtained the data for every 40-year period from 1928 through 2019 (there were 78 of them). The average 40-year return for small-company stocks was 13.8%, which would turn $10,000 into $1,760,721, nearly **three times** as much as the S&P 500 ($650,009), which grew at 11%.

Another striking piece of data popped up in this study: The **worst** 40-year period for small-company stocks was only slightly below the **average** 40-year return of the S&P 500.

## The fine print

As a bit of "fine print" to this discussion, we should point out that there's no official definition of exactly what constitutes a small-company stock.

As noted in our glossary, small-company stocks are generally regarded as having an average market capitalization of less than $3 billion. (Market capitalization is the current share price multiplied by the total number of shares outstanding, or the theoretical market value of an entire company. Small-company stocks are commonly referred to as "small caps.")

As the basis of the statistics in this book, we use an index of companies with an average market capitalization of $1.6 billion.

Large-company stocks have an average market capitalization of over $15 billion.

Our main point is that however you define them, over long periods small-company stocks have a record of producing higher returns than their larger counterparts. We think they should play a significant role in your investments.

And if you adopt our suggestions for a Two Funds for Life portfolio, they will!

# 8.

# Small Step #8
# **Invest in Value Stocks**

*"The secret to investing is to figure out the value of something—and then pay a lot less."*
Joel Greenblatt: author, The Little Book That Beats the Market

Okay, you ask, what's a "value" stock? Good question.

Recalling the previous chapter, just as a small company is defined by contrast to a large company, a value stock is defined in contrast to a growth stock.

A typical growth stock is likely to be one that most big investors regard highly for various reasons. These can include a top-notch earnings record and potential, a high market share within its industry, outstanding management, and stellar prospects. In short, a growth company is what many people think of as an "excellent" company.

Companies like this made it onto those "Nifty 50" lists in the 1970s.

Nothing wrong with that, right?

Right—except for one little detail: A popular stock like that is priced accordingly. You'll rarely be able to buy it at a bargain price because everybody already knows everything good about it.

We're not saying there's anything wrong with buying popular growth companies. But read on.

## The value of being "unexcellent"

Value companies, you could say, are "unexcellent" ones. Often there is nothing fundamentally wrong with them, and many of them have familiar household names and products.

But for whatever reason, they are not the darlings of institutional investors.

- Maybe their market share is slipping, or their products are on the way out, to be replaced by something newer.

- Maybe they have suboptimal management, or they're saddled with debt or gigantic legal troubles.
- Maybe these companies just don't generate enough excitement among investors.
- Maybe they're in for—or overdue for—a corporate turnaround.

For these and many other reasons, value companies aren't nearly as pricey as the popular growth companies.

## Buy low, sell high

There's less demand for value stocks. Less demand means lower prices. Lower prices can mean bargain prices. Bargain prices for value stocks let investors do what they know they should be doing, i.e., buying low, as in the old saying "buy low, sell high."

As with small companies, value companies should be owned by the hundreds, ideally in index funds. You'll find plenty of familiar names among the largest holdings of Vanguard's Value Index Fund, including Berkshire Hathaway, Johnson & Johnson, Exxon Mobil, Proctor & Gamble, JPMorgan Chase, and Bank of America.

Here's a very valid question: How in the world could such well-known companies wind up as relatively underpriced bargains?

Stock indexes are built on statistics, not judgments or opinions.

If you want to know where a stock falls on the scale of growth (expensive) to value (cheaper), there's a simple way to tell. It's called the price-to-earnings ratio, and it measures how much investors are currently willing to pay for every dollar of current profit.

## Amazon vs. Bank of America

Let's compare two well known corporate giants: Amazon, a renowned growth company, and Bank of America, one of the country's largest banks.

As we write this, Amazon's stock price is 115.7 times its earnings per share. That means investors are so confident in Amazon's future that they are willing to pay more than $115 for every dollar the company is currently earning. The rationale: Future earnings will grow so much that in the future, today's price will seem like a bargain.

At the same time, Bank of America's stock price is only 10.2 times its earnings per share.

Those numbers, 115.5 and 10.2, are known as the price/earnings (P/E) ratios of the two stocks. That ratio is a reliable way to compare companies regardless of their size and the industries in which they do business.

(As we write this, the P/E ratio of the U.S. stock market as a whole, represented by the S&P 500, is 21.9).

So why buy value companies? Because you can buy them at what may turn out to be bargain prices. If you buy value stocks by the hundreds, through a mutual fund, they are a good long-term bet for part of an equity portfolio.

Reliable data on value stocks goes back to 1928. An index of value stocks from 1928 through 2019 had a compound return of 11.1%, compared with 9.9% for the S&P 500.

Since 1928, value stocks were profitable in three out of every four calendar years.

Savvy young investors should be more interested in 40-year periods. And the news there is good. The average 40-year return of large-company value stocks was 13.5%, compared with 10.9% for the S&P 500.

That qualifies this step to potentially add $1 million to your portfolio.

There's no question in our minds that value stocks have something quite valuable to add to an equity portfolio. And they play a key role in our Two Funds for Life strategy.

9.

# Small Step #9

# **Buy and Hold**

*"I've said 'stay-the-course' a thousand times,*
*and I meant it every time."*
John C. Bogle

This step is especially easy because it tells you to do nothing instead of doing something.

Well, maybe it's not as easy as it sounds. Otherwise, why would we even have to mention it?

From you, the reader, to us, the authors: Okay, how in the heck can you argue that doing nothing is worth a $1 million payoff? Have you already gone off the deep end so early in the book?

From us, the authors, to you, the reader: Only our psychiatrists know for sure!

We regard this as a million-dollar step because if you don't follow it, you could easily lose $1 million over your investing lifetime.

This is so important that we'll elaborate a bit.

The **opposite** of buying and holding is sometimes called market timing—and it's what you should **not** do. It involves buying and selling when you think the time is right to take advantage of the market's ups and downs.

Unfortunately, the overwhelming majority of attempts at market timing are counterproductive.

As you invest your hard-earned savings over the years, it's all but guaranteed that there will be times when you just "know"—or at least seriously worry—that the stock market is no longer a safe place for your money.

At those times, many investors will be bailing out of the market and putting their money into the safety of cash or bonds, or even Bitcoin or perhaps something entirely new.

Commentators will bemoan the economy's weakness, and you could easily come to believe that you should bail out too.

Don't do market timing. Think about the possibility that bailing out could cost you $1 million. Then just say no thanks.

# I just can't take it anymore!

The most popular market timing system is one that we call "I Can't Stand It Anymore!" It kicks in when your portfolio is going down and you're getting nervous, afraid, or upset.

Here's how it often works:

Think of the letter "V" as representing the line of a graph of the stock market, from left to right. The market starts high then heads downward. You get nervous. It keeps going down.

When you look at the letter "V," you can see that it has a bottom point, after which the market changes course and goes back up.

But in real life, you can never see that future. All you see is a line heading straight down into an abyss. Your gloomy view seems to be validated by all the attention it gets in the media.

When your emotional pain reaches the breaking point, you get that "I Can't Stand It Anymore!" feeling. You throw up your hands, tell yourself you are "cutting your losses," and you sell.

Immediately you feel a sense of relief. As the market continues to slide, you feel smart, and at the same time, you feel sorry for all those suckers who didn't have your good sense.

But then at some point, the market reaches what looks like the bottom of a "V" (usually it isn't nearly as obvious as the letter would make it seem) and starts to go back up.

What do you do now? If you knew that the market had hit bottom and was about to head back up and reach (and then exceed) its former peak, you would jump back in. But you're wary, and the financial media continues to make you nervous. So you keep your money in cash.

As the market **keeps** going up, commentators gradually get more optimistic. You see stock market gains on the news almost every day. You know people who say they're making money. You start to think you're missing out.

But here's the bald-face truth: You will get absolutely no signal to alert you to the perfect time to get back in. In hindsight, you'll see that the very best time would have been at the bottom of the "V." But you'll never be able to identify that point until it's long past.

What should you do? Finally, maybe even after the market is well above the point at which you sold, you reach your emotional limit. Biting your tongue, you buy back in—at prices that are higher than they were when you sold.

You feel like a chump, but at least you'll be able to benefit from future gains.

## Selling low, buying high

In the scenario we just outlined, your emotions lured you into doing the opposite of what investors **should** do, which is buy low and sell high. You sold your investments and then repurchased them at a higher price.

That's the problem with the "I Can't Stand It Anymore!" timing system: It gives you temporary emotional comfort, but also long-term financial pain.

If you think we're exaggerating, or referring to only a few misguided individuals, consider this: A rigorous study of investor behavior that's been ongoing for 36 years has concluded, time after time, that the average individual investor fails to achieve not only the returns of the stock market, but even the returns of the mutual funds in which they invest.

We wrote about this previously, and an online search for "Paul Merriman" and the word "DALBAR" will turn up a good article about how investors shoot themselves in the foot, so to speak.

Here's the summary: studying investors' decisions about when to buy, sell, and exchange mutual funds, a Boston research firm named DALBAR has found that investors, often on the advice of their advisors and brokers, have given up billions of dollars in gains by making short-sighted decisions.

One key finding of the study is that investors who buy and hang on are consistently more successful than those who move in and out of the markets.

In its 2020 report, DALBAR said 20 years of data (2000 through 2019) indicated that the S&P 500 had an annual compound return of 6.06%, yet the average investor in equity mutual funds achieved a compound return of only 4.25% because many investors buy and sell instead of staying the course.

In other words, actual investors earned only 70% of what they could have earned very easily—by doing nothing at all.

## It's even worse

That's bad enough, but the word "average" means lots of investors did not even do that well. They thought at the time they were doing the right things. But they weren't, and they paid a high price.

The lesson from all the data in this long-term study is crystal clear: If you properly allocate your investments and then hang onto them through thick and thin, you are highly likely to get above-average returns.

This doesn't mean you'll "beat the market" or the indexes. But it does mean your returns will be above the average of all investors.

## A real-world demonstration

In what is sometimes called the Great Recession, this pattern played out for many people, quite possibly including your parents or some of their contemporaries.

The year 2008 was particularly distressing for the stock market, and millions of people bailed out. When the market roared back starting in 2009, they missed out.

Worse, as the market kept going up (eventually leading to one of the longest and strongest bull markets in history), their pain kept getting worse as they realized they would have to pay increasingly higher prices for stocks.

## Could have been much better

Many of those investors were so badly burned (by what they would describe as the behavior of the market and what we would describe as their counterproductive behavior) that they never got back into the stock market at all and missed the huge U.S. stock market opportunity of 2009–2017. That 10-year period didn't include even one losing year, but it **did** have seven years of double-digit gains and a compound return of 15.3%, enough to turn $10,000 into $36,013.

Some people regard market timing as a defensive strategy against bear markets. But a much better way to defend your money is by holding an appropriate part of your portfolio in fixed-income funds.

And if you follow our recommendations in this book, you will do that. You'll do it automatically and without having to think about it.

That way, you'll be free to take this Small Step by buying and holding.

Before we leave, consider for a moment this interesting question:

Is there ever a reliable way to "time" the market to your advantage? As it turns out, there is!

That's the topic of Chapter 10.

# 10.

## Small Step #10

# Put Simple Math to Work for You

*"With dollar-cost averaging, you take a lot of the emotion and fear out of investing because where the market goes in the short-term is far less important to you, as long as you stick to a regular investment plan."*
Nerd Wallet: a popular financial web site.

If the description of this step, "dollar-cost averaging," makes you think of some obscure formula that requires college mathematics to understand, relax! If you're regularly saving money, this is easy to understand and easy to do.

The formula is simple: Set up regular savings, ideally through payroll deduction or some other automatic method, and invest the same number of dollars every time. That's it.

That's really all? Yes, that's all there is to it.

To see how it works, imagine that you're adding $100 every month to a mutual fund with a price that varies every business day.

In the following example, we will exaggerate the potential ups and downs of that mutual fund price so you can see how this works in your favor.

The following table shows four monthly investments of $100 each at four different fund prices. Notice that when the price is lower, your $100 buys more shares, and when it's higher, you buy fewer shares.

## Automatic. Done!

This happens automatically with no thought or effort needed from you.

**Table 10-1:** Dollar-cost averaging

| Month | January | February | March | April |
|---|---|---|---|---|
| You invested | $100 | $100 | $100 | $100 |
| Fund price | $20 | $15 | $18 | $24 |
| Shares you buy | 5 | 6.67 | 5.55 | 4.17 |
| Shares you own | 5 | 11.67 | 17.23 | 21.4 |
| Your total cost | $100 | $200 | $300 | $400 |
| Your cost per share | $20 | $17.14 | $17.41 | $18.69 |
| Average of all prices | $20 | $17.50 | $17.67 | $19.25 |

Here's what that bottom right-hand corner of the table shows: You paid $18.69 for each share of that fund you now own. That is noticeably less than the average of all four prices ($19.25).

Dollar-cost averaging won't guarantee you a profit. It won't guarantee that the fund you invest in is a good one for you.

But this Small Step WILL guarantee that your cost for the shares you own will be lower than the average of all the prices you pay.

If you think this is sort of ho-hum, here's a little story to show why this can really, really matter.

# Doing the impossible

For small-company value stocks, the 10-year period from 1929 through 1938 was pretty dreadful. If you invested $1,000 at the start of 1929 and did nothing else, by the end of 1938, you would have had only $480 left. Your loss would have been 52%.

But if you had used dollar-cost averaging and invested $100 at the start of each of those 10 years, you would have ended 1938 with a profit. Instead of losing $520, you would have made $524.

Why this huge difference? Mostly because small-company value stocks had wild annual ups and downs. This made it unlikely any investor would calmly keep investing year after year. But for anybody who did, the year-by-year losses provided opportunities to buy assets on the cheap.

**Table 10-2**: Small-cap value index returns

| Year | Return |
|------|--------|
| 1929 | -37.1% |
| 1930 | -43.6% |
| 1931 | -55.5% |
| 1932 | -10.5% |
| 1933 | +125% |
| 1934 | -6.3% |
| 1935 | +47.7% |
| 1936 | +66.5% |
| 1937 | -50.6% |
| 1938 | +32.6% |

In 1933, 1935, 1936, and 1938, all the cheaply purchased shares available after the declines of 1929 through 1932 were there to benefit from huge double-digit returns.

This certainly is an unusual case, but it shows something that's well worth knowing: Regular investments using dollar-cost averaging in a group of stocks with greatly fluctuating prices can turn a losing investment into a winning one.

You probably won't ever have to face a market with that much volatility. However, this extreme example shows that dollar-cost averaging (when it is coupled with a level of patience that would have seemed wildly unreasonable) can work wonders.

Though we don't know the future, we can guarantee that there will never be a reliable signal that tells you the best time has arrived to get into the market. There will always be signs of potential trouble ahead.

If you wait until everything looks positive, you'll wait too long for any bargains, and you'll lose your greatest opportunities.

Dollar-cost averaging makes you more likely to succeed as an investor by forcing you to buy more of an asset when the price is relatively low.

In the long run, this practice rewards faith and discipline.

If dollar-cost averaging reduces or eliminates your desire to tinker with timing your investments, it certainly could be a $1 million step.

And if you're regularly saving money through payroll deductions, this is something you're probably already doing without having to even think about it.

Remember, we said this is easy!

# 11.

## Small Step #11

# Minimize the Drag of Taxes

*"A fine is a tax for doing something wrong.*
*A tax is a fine for doing something right."*
Anonymous

It's been said many times: No matter what you do, you can't escape death and taxes. But you don't have to overpay, and that's what this is chapter is about.

We believe everyone has a duty to pay their fair share of taxes; it's like paying your part of the rent.

But here's a problem: Millions of investors don't take the trouble to think about the tax implications of what they do. That neglect can cost a lot of money— potentially millions of dollars for people with enough assets.

Taxes are complex, and the first draft of this chapter was much longer than what you see here (you're welcome).

However, there are a few basic principles you should not ignore. At the end of this chapter, we'll suggest one specific Small Step you can take that will cover most, if not all, of this territory for you.

Two major issues might seem like technicalities when you're young and don't have much money. But they will probably make a big difference to you later.

One issue is the difference between accounts that are fully taxed and accounts that get favorable tax treatment.

The second issue, assuming you open a tax-favored account, is the difference between a traditional account (tax-deferred) and a Roth account (tax-free).

## Types of accounts

The first big divide is between taxable accounts and tax-sheltered accounts.

You probably have a bank account that includes savings and checking, and you might earn a little interest (probably *very* little) on your savings account balance. That interest is taxable income to you, and your bank sends you a form every year telling how much interest income the bank has reported to the Internal Revenue Service.

Similarly, you can open a regular investment account at a brokerage firm or a mutual fund company, and the earnings will be taxable to you every year.

These are taxable accounts, and as far as the IRS is concerned, there's no limit to how much you can put in or take out. For short- and medium-term goals like saving up for a vacation or a new car, these are the accounts to use.

But for retirement savings, you should put your money in a tax-sheltered account such as a 401(k) or similar plan through your work or in an Individual Retirement Account (IRA). Ideally, you will do both.

Because those accounts give you tax advantages, they come with restrictions on how much (and when) you can add money and on when you can start taking your money out without paying a penalty. (If you take that money back before you're 59½ years old, you may have to pay a 10% penalty.)

The main point to remember is that when you're saving for retirement, you should put as much money as you can into tax-advantaged accounts.

## Traditional vs. Roth

IRAs and 401(k) accounts come in two varieties, traditional and Roth. The differences involve taxes and restrictions. Inside either type, your investments will likely earn dividends and capital gains.

## Traditional

In a traditional IRA or 401(k), you invest money and take a tax deduction for your investment. Add $5,000, then deduct that $5,000 from your taxable income. Nice!

In this type of account, you will eventually owe taxes on all the money that you take out. But in the meantime, you get to keep all your dividends and capital gains working for you, along with your own investments.

The advantage of this arrangement is that you can deduct your contributions. If your highest tax rate is 12% and you contribute $5,000, you get a tax break of $600. That means the contribution effectively costs you only $4,400.

And though you'll have to pay taxes someday on that $5,000, that $600 you would otherwise have paid in taxes keeps working for you.

In the presumably far-distant future, when you are ready to take money out of your account, whatever you withdraw will be treated as taxable income. There's still a potential benefit to this because you could be in a lower tax bracket after you stop working.

## Roth

In a Roth account, you don't get a tax deduction for money you contribute. Sure, that's a bummer! But it has a silver lining: You will never pay taxes on anything you withdraw from a Roth account, as long as you abide by a few restrictions on when you take money out.

That means all the money you make inside a Roth IRA or a Roth 401(k) is truly tax-free.

There's another important benefit from a Roth account. It might not seem like much now, but you are likely to thoroughly appreciate it when you're retired.

With a traditional account, the IRS won't forget that you have not yet paid taxes on the money you invested and the money you earned. Eventually (currently the law says this is the year you turn 72), you will be required to withdraw—and pay taxes on—at least a prescribed percentage of your account balance every year. This is how the government makes sure it eventually gets its money.

This rule is called a "required minimum distribution," and every advisor, bank, brokerage house, mutual fund company, and 401(k) administrator is familiar with it.

But in a Roth account, there is no required minimum distribution. None. Because the government isn't going to collect any taxes on what you withdraw, it doesn't require you to take any money out.

The upshot is that with a Roth account, you can keep your money earning tax-free income for as long as you like. This gives you a lot more flexibility when you're retired. It may not seem like a big deal now, but we promise that if you have that flexibility later, you will appreciate it.

To sum up this discussion, you have a choice of account types:

- Taxable account
- Traditional IRA or 401(k)
- Roth IRA or 401(k)

That choice matters more than it might seem.

Choosing a Roth IRA or a Roth 401(k) will save you taxes in the future. It is quite possible that tax rates will be much higher in 40 years than they are now. That would certainly magnify the value of having a Roth account.

## A very smart step

Here's the Small Step of this chapter: You don't have to be an expert on taxes. You just have to know one. When you're about to make an important financial decision, ask your tax advisor: "Is there a potential tax trap here that I should know about?"

Doing that could easily be worth $1 million or more.

12.

## Small Step #12

# Use a Target date Retirement Fund

*"Target date funds are a 'set it and forget it'
retirement savings option that removes two
headaches for investors: Deciding on a mix of assets
and rebalancing those investments over time."*
Nerd Wallet

We hesitate to call this a Small Step because its implications are huge. In a way, it's the granddaddy of the Small Steps.

And it comes with a grand bonus: If you take this step, you will automatically do nearly everything that we have prescribed so far.

Unfortunately, taking this step won't force you to save money, and it won't force you to start saving early (Small Steps #1 and #2). Those are up to you.

But if you invest in a target date retirement fund, which we'll describe in more detail in Chapter 14, you will automatically do a lot of the right things:

- You will invest in stocks (Small Step #3)
- You will invest in hundreds or even thousands of stocks, not just a few (Small Step #4)
- You will have low expenses (Small Step #5)
- You will invest in index funds (Small Step #6)
- You will invest in small-company stocks (Small Step #7)
- You will invest in value stocks (Small Step #8).
- You will avoid trying to time the market (Small Step #9)
- You will get the benefit of dollar-cost averaging if you buy this fund through payroll deduction or automatic deposits to a savings account (Small Step #10)
- You will avoid high taxes (Small Step #11).

That's a lot in one package!

So what is this miraculous thing called a target date retirement fund?

Basically, it's a mutual fund that invests in other mutual funds and is managed to gradually reduce your risk of stock exposure as you get closer to your planned retirement date.

## What's your target?

Every target date retirement fund has a year in its title. For example, the Vanguard Target Retirement 2055 Fund is considered to be suitable for somebody who hopes to retire within a few years of 2055.

Typically, these funds are named at five-year intervals (and managed accordingly). Vanguard, Fidelity, T. Rowe Price, Charles Schwab, and others have funds labeled for target years 2030, 2035, 2040, and so forth.

A target date fund will make sure you do most of the important things well while you avoid the huge mistakes so many investors make. You're more likely to get where you want to go if you use a target date fund than if you try to take all these Small Steps on your own.

There's more good news: If you follow the recommendations in the rest of this book, you will have all these benefits.

Is this worth $1 million? You bet!

# 13.

# Small Step #13:
## What's Ahead in This Book

*"Money is a guarantee that in the future we may satisfy a new desire when it arises."*
Aristotle

By this point, we hope you are eager to find out how you can put these Small Steps to work and achieve superior long-term results.

Before you turn to the next section, here's a hint of what's coming.

You know the value of investing in small-company stocks (Small Step #7) and value stocks (Small Step #8). There's another stock type that combines the merits of these two: It's called small-company value, and we'll discuss it in Chapter 16.

You've been introduced to the advantages of a target date retirement fund, which we discuss further in Chapter 14.

When we get to the implementation stage, we'll show you a simple two-fund strategy that, over time, will let you take advantage of small-company value investing. (If you're skittish, we'll also show you how to get much of that same advantage while taking somewhat less risk.)

## A sneak preview

Here's a peek at one way to do that: Imagine you're young and you can commit to investing $1,000 a year for 40 years.

You consider two possibilities.

**ONE**: You could invest all your money in the Standard & Poor's 500 Index. Based on the average 40-year return of that index from 1928 through 2019 (11%), after 40 years, your savings would grow to $581,826—a very nice result from the $40,000 that you saved over the years.

**TWO**: Alternatively, you could take a small leap of faith into small-company value stocks by allocating 10% of each annual investment ($100 a year) to a small-company value fund, putting the other 90% in the S&P 500.

Again, based on average 40-year returns since 1928 (16.2% for small-company value stocks), that second strategy would be worth $759,670 after 40 years. That's about 30% more than you would have from the S&P 500 by itself.

That difference came from doing something different with only $100 a year, or only 10% of your portfolio.

The payoff from this Small Step is nearly *five times* as much as the total of *all the money* that you put in over 40 years.

In Section Three of this book, we'll look at other (and in our opinion, even better) ways you can combine two funds to achieve your goals—and quite possibly exceed them.

# Section Two
# BUILDING BLOCKS

# 14.

# A Young Investor's Best Friend: The Target-Date Fund

*"When there are multiple solutions to a problem, choose the simplest one."*
John C. Bogle

*Authors' note: This is the longest chapter in this book. But in some ways, it's the most important. Paragraph for paragraph, we don't know anywhere you'll get more benefit from the time it takes you to read this.*

Two Funds for Life uses a target date retirement fund, a product that we introduced briefly in Chapter 12 and will be the backbone of your portfolio. If you use it well, it will be amazingly valuable to you.

In 2020, researchers at the University of Pennsylvania's Wharton School of Business concluded that 401(k) investors who put their money in target date funds earned an average of 2.3 percentage points more than investors who used the other mutual funds in their retirement plans instead.

Involving over one million participants in 880 plans that offered Vanguard target date funds, the study covered a 12-year period ending in 2015 that included strong market growth as well as the severe bear market of 2007–2009.

Over 30 years, the researchers concluded that difference could translate into 50% more retirement wealth for participants who invest solely in target date funds than those who invest in other funds offered in their plans.

Many people will make investments they will hold longer than 30 years, and for them, this benefit will be larger.

Think for a moment about those 2.3 extra percentage points of annualized return from a target date fund.

In Chapter 4, we saw that a difference of just 0.5% could add more than $1 million to your lifetime investment results. This study is saying a target-date fund is more than four times as powerful.

Do we have your full attention? If so, let's dig into the details.

To understand a target date fund, you should be familiar with two products: The mutual fund and the index fund.

## The mutual fund

A mutual fund is an investment pool that treats ordinary folks almost the same as wealthy investors. Nowadays, even the most ignorant, uninterested, and naïve investor (obviously we're not saying this applies to you!) can get fair and reasonably priced professional treatment from Wall Street.

It wasn't always like that.

Before the mutual fund was invented (the first one was the Massachusetts Investors Trust, started in 1924), the investment world was organized primarily to benefit wealthy individuals who had lots of resources as well as the trust departments of banks and old-school brokerage firms that charged fees and commissions to buy and sell individual stocks and bonds.

Some of these banks and investment firms eventually figured out that it would be in their interest to find an efficient way to help the children and other family members of their wealthy clients. The solution they found was a private arrangement for pooling money and sharing the costs of professional management. Thus was born the in-house mutual fund.

Before long, Wall Street realized that money could be made by offering this arrangement to the public, and that led to the mutual fund as we know it today.

The advantages of mutual funds are no secret. By pooling your money with that of many other shareholders, you can get broad diversification (Small Step #4) and yet start with a very small investment; in some cases, their minimum initial investment is as low as $1.

It's easy to buy and sell mutual fund shares. At the end of every business day, you can sell your shares back to the mutual fund company (or buy more) at the exact price they are worth that day—your proportional share of all the underlying securities and cash in the fund's portfolio.

As a mutual fund shareholder, you get professional management and access to stocks and other investment products at low costs that would be difficult, if not impossible, for most individuals to achieve.

Most mutual funds make it easy for you to automatically have dividends and capital gains reinvested, to make periodic additions to your accounts, and to make automatic withdrawals.

Because mutual funds are subject to government regulation and have to report their key information in standard ways, it is easy to compare them.

Is this a perfect investment vehicle? Not quite.

- Mutual funds don't let shareholders in taxable accounts control the timing of capital gains and losses. Shareholders can be stuck with unexpected tax bills as a result, although usually these bills are modest.
- Fund managers may actively buy and sell securities, creating taxable income for shareholders, even if the shareholders don't do any trading themselves.
- Worse, mutual fund expenses can be very high, often taking away one to two percentage points of the return that a fund's portfolio earned for shareholders.

All these things added up to a lucrative business for companies that managed mutual funds. But they weren't always optimal for fund shareholders.

## The index fund

The second essential building block of a properly designed target-date fund is the index fund (we say "properly" because we believe investors should avoid target date funds that are built of actively managed funds instead of index funds).

Stock indexes like the Standard & Poor's 500 Index have been around for many decades. Long ago, big institutional investors devised low-cost ways to buy most or all the stocks in an index, creating their own private funds. These pools were called index funds.

John Bogle, the founder of The Vanguard Group (now one of the largest mutual fund companies), dealt a shock to the mutual fund industry in 1976 by offering an index fund for sale to the public.

Suddenly, individual investors could bypass high-priced managers and own virtually every stock within an asset class such as the S&P 500. Fund expenses could be cut to the bone—often by 90% or more—and taxable events could be minimized.

This offered investors more diversification, lower costs, lower risks, lower taxes and professional management all in a single package.

Many mutual funds still charged sales commissions that, in some cases, amounted to more than 9% of the money that was actually invested.

In 1977, Vanguard dropped sales charges on all its mutual funds, including index funds. That was a real boon to individual investors.

As you can imagine, not everybody was happy with this new development. For years, Wall Street tried to fight index funds.

But as more and more individual investors started realizing that index funds were a low-cost ticket to better returns, Wall Street caved, deciding to embrace the trend rather than resist it.

Over the past 40 years, index funds have found widespread acceptance. Costs to shareholders have dropped, in a few cases to zero. Index funds now hold trillions of dollars in investment assets for individuals, corporations, and other institutions.

Although the first index funds concentrated on

large-company stocks like those in the S&P 500 Index, there are now separate index funds for enough types of U.S. and international stocks that ordinary investors can custom-tailor their portfolios to their individual needs.

## Not quite perfect

Although index funds almost always do a fine job of tracking the performance of their index, they have no way to meet the individual needs of their shareholders.

Most people saving for retirement need what we call a "glide path"—a plan for gradually reducing their overall level of risk as they grow older. Index funds don't have any such glide path, which is their biggest shortcoming for most investors.

One or more all-equity index funds might be suitable for investors in their 20s and 30s. But by the time most investors reach their 40s or 50s, they should also own some bond funds to reduce their portfolio's volatility.

Ideally, the proportion of stocks in your portfolio should come down gradually as you approach retirement. But index funds don't make any provision for that.

Of course, it's not hard to create your own glide path by making changes over time. For example, you can sell some shares of an equity index fund and put the proceeds into a fixed-income index fund.

But this requires you to make a decision and take action to implement it. Unfortunately, the majority of investors do those things poorly, too late, or not at all.

A new product to the rescue!

# The target-date retirement fund

In the late 20th century, as corporate pensions fell by the wayside and individual investors were increasingly required to make their own investment choices inside their 401(k) and other retirement plans, most participants in those plans made one initial decision— then never reviewed their allocations over time, even as their risk tolerance evolved.

Some investors left all their money in "safe" options like money-market funds, therefore getting very little return. Others put all their money in equities and left it there until they retired. Neither of those approaches was wise.

The solution began to take shape in the early 1990s when Wells Fargo and Barclays Global Investors figured out that they could provide a lifelong strategy that would suit most investors. Their strategy: Organize the participants in retirement plans into groups with broadly similar needs.

The two companies realized that the most powerful piece of data about any given investor was the number of years remaining before the expected start of retirement, so they introduced the first target date fund in 1994.

(Here's a hint of what's ahead: That data point, i.e., the number of years before retirement, is an important part of Two Funds for Life.)

Most people who expected to retire in any given year would presumably be well served by a similar glide path, which could be provided by a specific mix of stocks and bonds.

For example, people who plan to retire within a few years of 2050 presumably have similar needs for gradually reducing their investment risk.

Over the years within a "2050" fund, the managers can gradually reduce the proportion of equity funds while they gradually increase the proportion of fixed-income funds.

A "2030" fund will be managed much more conservatively since its shareholders presumably plan to retire much sooner. These people, less than a decade away from retirement, presumably cannot afford to have the bulk of their money in stocks, since a major market decline could wipe out enough value that they could be forced to delay their retirement.

# A terrific product in many ways

For investors who want to make just one investment decision that is likely to serve them well for the rest of their lives, a target date fund seemed like an excellent choice.

The public quickly agreed. Fidelity introduced its Freedom Funds in 1996; T. Rowe Price followed in 2002, and Vanguard in 2003.

Vanguard is now by far the largest player in this market, managing almost 40% of all the assets in target-date funds—more than the second-, third-, and fourth-largest providers combined.

According to Vanguard, roughly half of all 401(k) retirement plan participants have their entire accounts in just one target date fund as their default investment strategy.

In other words, American workers are relying very heavily on these funds for their futures. It's not a tremendous stretch to say that the target-date fund has taken the place once held by the corporate pension.

Target date funds have total assets measured in trillions of dollars. We believe they are among the greatest modern financial inventions that benefit individual investors. For an investment product that's not yet 25 years old, that's pretty impressive.

## Still not quite perfect

Still, target date funds don't go the whole distance in taking care of investors.

Here are four ways they fall short.

**Problem #1:** Large-company blend stocks often make up about 75% of the equity component of a typical target-date fund. This means the funds fail to give investors significant access to some long-established stock types with superior long-term track records.

Specifically, target date funds have only minimal exposure to small-company stocks (Small Step #7) and value stocks (Small Step #8). Over the years, these two types of stocks have consistently achieved significantly higher long-term returns than large-company blend funds that include growth stocks and value stocks.

As a result, long-term investors in target date funds miss out on returns that could potentially double the amount of money they will have to spend during their retirement years.

We believe that 20-something investors can safely benefit from having at least half their money in small-company stocks and value stocks. Target date funds don't give them anything remotely close to that.

**Problem #2:** There's little disagreement that young investors can afford to take more risks than older investors, and they have ample time to reap the likely long-term rewards of doing so. Yet target date funds use the same mix of stocks for all investors regardless of their age.

Target date funds provide only one type of glide path: By gradually reducing the portfolio's exposure to equity funds. They could easily provide another glide path by adjusting the mix of stocks, for example, by owning more value stocks and small-company stocks in the early years, then transitioning to more large-company blend stocks as retirement gets closer.

But target date funds don't do this.

**Problem #3:** Target date funds treat their shareholders as if the only thing that matters is their age. This is effective up to a point, and it's certainly convenient for fund companies.

However, by lumping everybody of a certain age into a single pool, target-date funds wind up with the appropriate mix of assets for only some of their shareholders, not all of them.

Some people are inherently adventurous (aggressive), and others inherently more skittish (conservative).

Fund companies could easily design three variants of each target date fund. For example: One for investors who prefer an aggressive approach, one for those who see themselves as moderate, and a third for investors who regard themselves as more conservative.

**Problem #4:** Target date funds saddle even their youngest shareholders with bonds, reducing their expected annual returns by approximately 0.5% for every 10 percentage points of the portfolio that are not in equities.

## The good news

Fortunately, Two Funds for Life provides a good solution to each of these shortcomings.

- It tackles Problem #1 by adding a healthy dose of small-company and value stocks.
- It tackles Problem #2 by offering a glide path that adjusts the risk of the types of stocks as well as the overall risk of holding equities.
- It tackles Problem #3 by prescribing a moderate option and then showing how to easily modify it for investors who are more aggressive or more conservative.
- It tackles Problem #4 by reducing (though not eliminating entirely) the bond component of young investors' portfolios.

To our great delight, and to your benefit, the strategy outlined in this book shows how you can get all these benefits from adding just one additional fund to your target date fund.

Hence the name: **Two Funds for Life**.

# 15.

# Risk in the Real World

*"Go out on a limb. That's where the fruit is."*
U.S. President Jimmy Carter

In Chapter 16, we'll dig into the type of stock that, in our opinion, has the best potential for beefing up the returns you're likely to achieve in your target date fund. We'll present our best recommendations for how you combine Two Funds for Life.

In the real world, things don't always turn out the way we want or expect them to. That certainly applies to investing money. So let's get the topic of **investment risk** out on the table right now for a short discussion.

This is a big topic, and we hope you will regard what follows as "just a little straight talk among friends" (to borrow a phrase from President Gerald Ford's speech when he took the oath of office).

Our recommendations will be most potent for young investors, i.e., those with decades left before they expect to retire. If you have lots of time ahead, you should ask yourself, What is the real risk I'm taking?

It's no secret that there's more statistical risk in small-company value stocks than in the S&P 500 or the mix of stocks that make up most target date funds.

To get on the same page, let's differentiate between "statistical risk" and what we call "real-world risk."

Statisticians like to fall back on standard deviation, which essentially measures predictability (or technically, the magnitude of variation in a set of numbers—in this case, investment returns over time).

A low standard deviation indicates that annual returns fall within a narrow band from highest to lowest. A low figure indicates the returns are quite predictable; a very high figure indicates they could be "all over the map."

That's useful if predictability is the most important thing to you. But in the real world, what scares investors is losing money. What they *want* is to make money.

If that's what you want, standard deviation is a poor guide.

Imagine an investment that year after year has annual returns in a narrow range, say between 9.5% and 10.5%.

That's quite predictable, with a low standard deviation that suggests it's not very risky.

Now imagine that every so often, the return falls into the range of 4% to 5%. That's much less predictable, and its higher standard deviation would label it relatively risky. You would probably agree.

But now imagine that those occasional returns were 14% or 15% instead. Would this seem risky to you? The formula for determining standard deviation makes no distinction between favorable and unfavorable variations. If it varies by much, it's unpredictable, and the statistic suggests it's risky.

In other words, the formula for standard deviation technically regards good fortune as just as "risky" as bad fortune.

We don't know anyone who thinks like that. The investors we know are happy to accept the best of times without getting scared. That's probably true for you, too.

That's why we put the phrase "in the real world" in the title of this chapter.

## Real-world risk

In the real world, a better way to think about risk is to consider what could happen that's bad, that could cost you money. What is the worst that's likely to happen?

If, like the majority of investors, you are no more than 55 years old, and thus you have at least a theoretical investment horizon of at least 40 years, you should be extremely interested in some numbers you'll find below in Tables 15-1 and 15-2.

With the help of a crack research team, we looked at the very **best** 40-year returns and the very **worst** 40-year returns for four major types of U.S. stocks: The Standard & Poor's 500 Index, large-company value stocks, small-company stocks (a blend of growth and value), and small-company value stocks.

To get right to the point, Table 15-1 shows that the worst 40-year period for each of three diversifying types of stock was better than the best 40-year period for the S&P 500 (read that again if you like).

**Table 15-1: Worst 40-year periods 1970–2019**

|  | Compound return |
|---|---|
| **Standard & Poor's 500 Index BEST** | 12.2% |
| **U.S. large-company value stocks WORST** | 13.1% |
| **U.S. small-company blend stocks WORST** | 12.5 % |
| **U.S. small-company value stocks WORST** | 15.4% |

For long-term investors, those numbers certainly show the benefit of diversifying beyond the Standard & Poor's 500 Index.

Now let's translate the numbers into dollars, assuming a one-time investment of $100.

Table 15-2 is identical to the previous one except that dollars are substituted for compound rates of return.

## Table 15-2: Worst 40-year periods, 1970–2019

|  | $100 grew to |
|---|---|
| **Standard & Poor's 500 Index BEST** | **$9,993** |
| **U.S. large-company value stocks WORST** | **$13,756** |
| **U.S. small-company blend stocks WORST** | **$11,120** |
| **U.S. small-company value stocks WORST** | **$30,777** |

In other words, among these four types of stocks, no matter what you did for any 40-year period from 1970 through 2019, you could not lose by diversifying beyond the Standard & Poor's 500 Index.

And that's essentially what we're suggesting in Two Funds for Life.

If your idea of risk is the probability of losing money, we hope you will remember this: In every 40-year period from 1970 through 2018, compared with the S&P 500, small-company value stocks gave investors much more of what they wanted (return) along with less of what they didn't want (risk).

If you want a reasonable shot at really superior performance, and if you've got faith and patience over a long time horizon, we believe your best choice is small-company value stocks.

In Chapter 16, we'll tell you more.

# 16.

# The Magic of Small-Company Value Stocks

*"There is magic, but you have to be the magician. You have to make the magic happen."*
Sidney Sheldon, novelist/writer/director/producer

Earlier in the book, we introduced small-company value stocks. These stocks effectively act like a turbo booster in the Two Funds for Life strategy.

As we saw, investing in small-company stocks has been very productive in the past. Smaller companies have lots of room to become big, and some of them grow exponentially. When you own them by the hundreds or thousands through a mutual fund or an exchange-traded fund, you'll be sure to own those relatively few small companies that are destined to become giants. That's where you're likely to make good money.

As we also saw, value stocks (those selling at "bargain" prices for various reasons) are good long-term investments when you own them by the hundreds or thousands. They have a long history of outperforming growth stocks, whether you're talking about small stocks or large ones, U.S. stocks, or international stocks. The value phenomenon holds up among emerging-markets stocks, too.

**We've seen that small works. We've seen that value works.**

It makes good sense to invest in both of these, and it makes terrific sense to combine the two by investing in small-company value stocks.

This is truly a 2-in-1 package deal: One asset class that combines the benefits of small size along with the bargain prices of value stocks. Over the past 92 years, small-company value has been a great addition to any equity portfolio.

It might seem like small-company value investing is doubly risky, and in some ways, it is. But in the long run, it has been amply rewarding, too. In Chapter 15, when we described the best and worst 40-year periods, we saw that for long-term investors, the risks of small-company value investing have been worthwhile.

Over the long haul, among the four major types of U.S. stocks (large-company blend, like the S&P 500, large-company value, small-company blend, and small-company value), the undisputed champion is small-company value. Let's look at some numbers.

One easy-to-understand way to measure "real-world risk" is to look at whether an investment was profitable or unprofitable in any particular calendar year.

From 1928 through 2019, small-company value stocks had 63 profitable calendar years, roughly two of every three. But that's only part of the story. In 45 of those years, the small-company value index was up more than 20%; and in 19 years, the gains were more than 40%.

Of course, there were negative years, roughly one of every three.

But if that statistic worries you, consider the following: On average, the positive years were twice as good as the negative years were bad. That means you got twice as many good years as bad ones, and on average the good years were very good.

In the last chapter, we explored returns in 40-year periods from 1970 through 2019.

Here, we want to take a longer view and look at 40-year returns from 1928 through 2019. That gives us a much bigger sample—52 such periods, in fact.

The very worst 40-year period began in 1928 and went through 1967. Small-company value stocks returned 11.6%, well above the 9.9% long-term return of the "safe" Standard & Poor's 500 Index.

Maybe 40 years is longer than you want to think about. OK, that's fair, so let's try 15 years. The very worst 15-year period for small-company value stocks started in 1928 and ended with a compound loss of 1.9%. The very best 15-year period began in 1975 and wound up with a compound gain of 26.3%.

On average, those 15-year periods brought gains of 16.2% to small-company value investors. Only seven of those periods resulted in compound returns below 10%.

There's no guarantee, of course, but we don't see any reason to doubt that small-company value stocks will continue to produce better long-term returns than the S&P 500.

One simple measure of the reward for taking risks is the compound rate of return. From 1928 through 2019, the S&P 500 compounded at 9.9%, while small-company value stocks compounded at 13.2%. That difference (13.2% vs. 9.9%) may not seem like much in just one year. But over a decade or several decades, it makes an enormous difference.

How enormous?

- Over 40 years, an investment growing at 9.9% (the S&P 500) would turn $1,000 into about $43,600.

- In that same period, a $1,000 investment growing at 13.2% (small-company value stocks) would turn $1,000 into about $142,500.

Although those numbers are impressive, they are the result of hindsight. We know how things turned out. But investors in real-time did not know that, and to achieve those rewards, they had to "stick with the plan" through thick and thin.

In real life, people look at their investments and evaluate their progress much more often than once every 40 years or so. There have been significantly long periods (and there will be more in the future) when large-company stocks did better than small-company stocks. Likewise, there were (and will be) periods when growth stocks do better than value stocks.

Risk, as it is actually experienced by investors, is subjective. When the widely followed Dow Jones Industrial Average and the Standard & Poor's 500 Index are going up, and your small-company-value fund is lagging behind, you may feel anxiety.

If you supplement your target date fund with small-company value stocks, you should expect that your two funds will often behave differently—maybe most of the time. Sometimes that difference will make you feel very smart or very lucky. Other times, that difference will make you feel unlucky or not so smart.

In Two Funds for Life, you look to small-company value funds for higher long-term returns. But you look to your target date fund for psychological solace. You'll perhaps get that solace in the comfortable knowledge that this important part of your portfolio is behaving "normally"—in other words, similarly to what you're likely hearing on the news.

If you can keep the faith, you'll benefit from the best of both worlds.

Paul Merriman and Richard Buck

# Section Three

# RECIPES FOR SUCCESS

▲

# 17.

# Two Funds for Life Before Retirement

*"Pearls don't lie on the seashore.*
*If you want one, you must dive for it."*
Chinese proverb

This chapter contains the specifics of our Two Funds for Life advice.

There's good news and bad news here. The bad news applies to us as authors; the good news applies to you.

The bad news: It's impossible to prescribe a lifetime of precisely suitable asset allocations for investors we don't know. And even if we know your current situation, we can't know the future, either the future of the markets or what steps you will take as an investor.

Therefore, we can't guarantee your results.

The good news: If your asset allocation is in the ballpark, you will have a high probability of long-term investing success.

## The simplest way to use this strategy

If you're looking for a one-decision way to get the benefits of a target date fund and small-company value stocks, without ever making any changes, here it is.

Allocate 90% of your current 401(k) balance, plus all future contributions, to your target date fund. Allocate the other 10% to a small-company value fund. Keep that allocation forever.

It can't get much simpler than that.

In every 40-year period from 1970 to 2019, this strategy produced a higher return than that of the target date fund alone. The results varied a lot depending on the starting point, but the average improvement over 40 years was 23%.

(If you want to ramp things up a notch, you could opt for 20% in small-company value instead of 10%. In those same 40-year periods, the average improvement was 45%.)

There's a downside to this. As you get older, your small-company value fund is likely to make up an increasingly large percentage of your portfolio, subjecting you to more and more risk. That's the opposite of the conventional wisdom that you should take less risk, not more, as you get older.

Fortunately, we can suggest a good way around that.

## Our basic advice

Nevertheless, our core advice is designed to remove that outsize risk in your retirement years. And it's almost as easy to implement.

The basic Two Funds for Life recommendation for your 401(k) plan is pretty simple:

- Multiply your age by 1.5.
- Use the result as the percentage of your portfolio that should be in a target date retirement fund. The rest goes into a small-company value fund.
- As you get older, rebalance these two funds periodically, ideally once a year, based on your age at the time. This will gradually reduce your small-company value exposure.

For example, if you are 30, multiply your age by 1.5 to get 45. That means 45% of your portfolio belongs in your target date fund; the other 55% goes into small-company value.

By that formula, when you're 40, you'll have 60% in the target date fund and 40% in small-company value.

When you're 50, you'll have 75% in the target-date fund and 25% in small-company value.

This approach is aggressive when you're young, and it becomes gradually less adventurous as you get older.

You may be wondering how much this will improve your portfolio results. We wanted to know that too, so we did some digging.

Using detailed data going back to 1970, we wanted to know how a target date fund all by itself would have fared in an average holding period of 40 years.

Because target date funds didn't exist until the 1990s, our research team built a model that used a glide path and asset allocations similar to those of Vanguard's target date funds.

We assumed an investor started with $1,000 and added another $1,000 (adjusted for actual inflation) for each of the next 39 years. We sliced and diced the data to compute the returns for hundreds of 40-year periods from 1970 through 2019 (we got hundreds of periods by simulating a different starting date at the beginning of every month).

The result: With all the money going into a target date fund, after 40 years, the average portfolio balance was $698,800.

Next, we asked what the average ending portfolio value would have been for an investor who followed our Two Funds for Life recommendations using a small-company value fund along with a target date fund.

The result: After the same 40 years of investments, that Two Funds for Life average portfolio value was $972,900.

The difference: $274,100, an increase of 39%.

Of course, we know that adding small-company value to a target date fund adds risk as well, so we asked our research team to measure the risk of these two investment plans during this hypothetically average 40-year period.

Specifically, we wanted to know the worst-ever drawdown in each case. (A drawdown is the percentage loss from a portfolio high to a subsequent low. For example, if the portfolio value peaked at $100,000 and then went down until it bottomed out at $80,000 before heading back up, the drawdown would be $20,000, or 20%.)

You might be surprised to learn that adding a small-company value fund to the target-date fund did not increase that risk by much. That's shown in Table 17-1.

# Table 17-1: Target date fund alone vs. Two Funds for Life, 1970–2019

|  | Vanguard-like target date fund | Two Funds for Life | Percentage change |
|---|---|---|---|
| **40-year growth of $1,000/year plus inflation** | $698,800 | $972,900 | +39% |
| **Worst-ever drawdown (risk)** | 41% | 49% | +20% |

## A less-risky alternative

We've designed this strategy to gradually reduce risk as your birthdays pile up.

But if you prefer a more conservative approach, it's easy: Substitute a large-company value fund for the small-company value fund. If you do that, you can expect lower volatility. And though you will forego the expected returns of small-company value stocks, you'll still get the impressive results of investing in value stocks (Small Step #8).

# Getting it just right

Unfortunately, it's impossible to know in advance the exact formula for achieving the highest returns. Your results will be unpredictable and out of your control.

Despite the best efforts of the smartest investors, the luck of timing plays a huge part in what happens. Here's an example, something we have both experienced in our lives as investors.

From 1975 through 1999, the Standard & Poor's 500 Index had a compound return of 17%. Small-company value stocks returned more than 22%.

But investors who might understandably have considered those returns "the new normal" were in for a rude awakening. From 2000 through 2019, the S&P 500's return was about 6%; small-company value stocks returned about 10%.

We began this book by urging investors to do two things: Save money and start saving earlier. Here's a third recommendation: Save more.

We know that's not possible for everyone, but in the face of such uncertainty, it's a good way to "hope for the best and plan for the worst."

# 18.

# Putting the Numbers to Work: Rebalancing

*"The beauty of periodic rebalancing is that it forces you to base your investing decisions on a simple, objective standard."*
Benjamin Graham, *The Intelligent Investor*

Rebalancing is the periodic chore of bringing your allocations back to their starting percentages.

For example, if your Two Funds for Life portfolio should be divided 50/50 between the two funds, and the small-company value part of it has grown to 55%, you can restore the prescribed percentages by selling some of the small-company value stocks and investing the proceeds in your target date fund.

How often should you rebalance?

The Two Funds for Life formula outlined in the previous chapter calls for rebalancing every year based on your age and expected retirement year. Once a year is standard practice: A long enough interval to give the higher-performing asset a chance to do its thing, but short enough to keep your risk level in check.

The choice of rebalancing frequency lets you fine-tune your level of risk. To choose less risk, rebalance more often. To allow more risk in hopes of achieving higher long-term returns, rebalance less often.

## Step-by-step

Rebalancing between just two funds is relatively easy. If you need step-by-step directions, here they are with a simple example.

**Step 1:** Determine your target allocation. Let's say your portfolio is worth $100,000, and your goal is to have 60% in your target date fund and 40% in your small-company value fund. That means your target date fund should have $60,000.

**Step 2:** Determine your actual allocation. Let's say your small-company value fund has grown so much that it's worth $48,000 (leaving your target date fund with only $52,000).

**Step 3:** Compute the difference between target and actual, in this case, $8,000. Sell that much of the fund that's gotten too big and reinvest that amount in the one that's too small.

Our recommendations assume your two funds are in a 401(k) or an IRA, in which case you'll not incur any tax consequences for selling some of your holdings in a fund and moving the proceeds to another.

If you're doing this in a taxable account, every sale of an appreciated asset may trigger a taxable gain. In this type of account, you'll keep more of your money working for you if you avoid selling anything. Especially in the early years, when your balances are smaller in relation to your regular contributions, you can reduce or eliminate the tax consequences if you leave the balances alone and allocate your contributions to the fund that's below its target.

However you do it, rebalancing will keep your portfolio on track. It's something you'll probably need to do even after you retire.

# 19.

# Two Funds After Retirement

*"Not everything that can be counted counts,*
*and not everything that counts can be counted."*
Albert Einstein

If you use the Two Funds for Life strategy to save enough money to retire, you have our hefty congratulations.

You may already know enough to figure out your investment needs from here on.

However, you most likely have a lot of years ahead of you as an investor. Some decisions you make now will affect you for the rest of your life, and they could affect your heirs as well.

In Chapter 20, we suggest some possible paths from which you can choose.

Before we get there, we have a little important homework for you, as well as a few questions for you to think about.

The most important piece of this homework should be done long before you actually retire.

The job is to figure out whether, when you retire, you have (or will have) "just barely enough" to support your needs or ample resources to live as you choose.

*Richard Buck: There's a middle ground that I sometimes describe as "We have enough to do what we want as long as we don't do something stupid."*

Calculating distributions (money you take out of your portfolio) is a vital part of retirement planning. It's beyond the scope of this book, but we'll take this opportunity to hit a few high points.

## What do you need?

If you've done a good job managing your investments, you're probably no slouch about the rest of your finances. You probably have a good idea in general of the regular expenses you can expect to continue.

Some expenses (commuting and buying work clothes, for example) will end. Some new expenses will arise, especially if your retirement dreams call for major travel or building a cabin at the lake.

**Step One:** Start by calculating the income you will need to maintain the lifestyle you desire in retirement.

You'll probably start with a mix of monthly, annual, or semiannual expenses like property taxes and variable expenses such as travel, gifts, and recreation.

When you've got these down, calculate this into an annual total.

# What will you have?

**Step Two:** Calculate whatever regular income you'll have from sources like Social Security, rental real estate, pensions, annuities, or interest on loans you might have made. Don't include capital gains or other investment income here (we'll get to that shortly).

Once you compute this annual non-investment income, you can easily compare it to your annual needs.

If the income you can count on is equal to or greater than your needs, you're in fabulous shape. More likely, however, you will need to draw from your portfolio to fully meet your needs. Think of the difference as a "gap."

**Step Three:** Calculate this annual gap as a percentage of your total investment portfolio, which may include investments in addition to your target date fund.

If, for example, your investments total $1 million and you need $40,000 from them per year to meet your needs, that gap is equal to 4% of your portfolio.

## Closing the gap

If you can close the gap and meet your needs by taking out 4% or less, then you're probably in good shape.

If you need to take out more than 4% of your portfolio each year to meet your needs, you should consider re-thinking your retirement plans. (This is why this step is particularly valuable when you have ample time before retirement.)

If you come up short, here are three options to consider:

- Postpone your retirement while you keep working and saving.
- Reduce your expectations for how much you'll spend.
- Plan to take on some part-time work during retirement, if possible.

You might find the best solution is a combination of two of those options—or even all three.

In any case, there's your homework.

## Things to think about

In addition, we think every new or soon-to-be retiree should spend some time thinking about a few basic questions:

- ➤ How important is it to leave money for kids, grandchildren, or charitable causes? Do you want to make sure there's likely to be money left in your estate for that?
- ➤ To meet your goals, are you willing to add one or even two additional funds to your target date fund?
- ➤ If you're hoping to leave money to your heirs, are you comfortable segregating that money and taking a bit more risk with it to potentially have a larger estate?

These questions will help you choose the path that's likely to do the best job of meeting your needs.

(What we have outlined here is a quick overview of a very important process that's described in Chapter 10 of our book *Financial Fitness Forever*. The chapter is called "Twelve Numbers to Change Your Life," and it's available free online at paulmerriman.com. To find it, search "twelve numbers to change your life.")

Next, we'll explore some of the possible paths that your answers might suggest.

20.

# Two Funds During Retirement

*"The goal of retirement is to
live off your assets—not on them."*
Frank Eberhart- author of The Sexy Little Book of Finance III

In the best possible scenario, your investments over a lifetime will have been so successful that your       target date fund will be worth more than enough to meet all your needs, and then some.

In this lovely case, your path could be ultra-simple: Keep your money in the target date fund and withdraw whatever you need to live the life you want without worrying about what's going on in the market.

## Six possible paths

But if you're not quite that fortunate, we have identified six possible paths you can follow, depending on your circumstances. You can mix and match them if you like, although we suspect that by now you enjoy the simplicity of owning just two funds. So don't let your creativity run away with you!

(This might be a good time to remind you of our advice in Chapter 11 regarding the need to pay attention to taxes. Before you embark on any of the suggested paths in this chapter, make sure you won't be inadvertently incurring large taxable capital gains.)

## Path One: If you have "enough"

If your portfolio can support 4% annual withdrawals, the conservatively allocated portfolio in your target date fund might be all you need.

It could be tempting to keep some of your money in a small-company value fund to potentially earn a higher return. But at this stage of your life, hanging on to what you have can be more important than potentially earning more.

Your best course could be to pare down your portfolio from two funds to just one. This will make your financial life simple and worry-free.

## Path Two: If you have "more than enough" and want a dependable income.

*Paul Merriman: When I talk to groups of retirees, I like to ask for a show of hands. How many people here have a pension? How many of you with your hands up get peace of mind from that pension? Usually, all the hands stay up.*

Most young people these days aren't likely to retire with corporate pensions. They may have Social Security, but the long-term future of that program is less than certain.

If your resources are ample, you can "buy" a pension in the form of an insurance contract called a single-premium life annuity. In return for an up-front payment based on your age and gender, the insurance company agrees to pay you monthly for the rest of your life, no matter how long you live.

Here's a simple Two Funds for Life strategy: "Buy a pension" that's large enough to meet your basic cash flow needs, then invest the remainder of your nest egg in another fund.

That could be your target date fund. Or it could be something with a bit more equity exposure that's likely to provide a higher long-term return.

Knowing that your basic needs are met by your annuity, you might be comfortable taking a bit more risk with the remainder of your portfolio.

Vanguard offers a group of "LifeStrategy" funds with lots of diversification and four choices of risk level.

Their annual expenses are very reasonable (Chapter Five), at just 0.13%.

These funds let you choose to have equities make up 20%, 40%, 60%, or 80% of your assets.

If you go that route, we'd suggest you first consider either 40% or 60% in equities, as those moderate allocations are not likely to get you in a lot of trouble.

*Paul Merriman: My wife and I have a 50/50 stock/bond mix in our retirement investments. You could easily accomplish that by making equal investments in the 40% LifeStrategy fund and its 60% counterpart.*

The proper allocation is entirely up to you and your comfort level.

## Path Three: If you want to make sure to take care of people or charities after you're gone.

If this is you, we suggest you set aside enough in your target date fund to amply support your own lifestyle in retirement, then choose another fund (or even more than one) with a level of risk that's appropriate for your heirs and intended beneficiaries.

Tossing out a number at random, imagine you have $200,000 that you doubt you will need in your lifetime, and you want to leave it to your daughter.

If you do nothing, "her" $200,000 inheritance could be tied up in a target date fund that by now is mostly invested in bonds (good for you, but not optimal for an investment that your daughter may not receive for 20 or more years).

You'll probably want to retain ownership of this money, of course, so you can tap into it in case you need to.

But there's no reason you can't invest that $200,000 in a way that will give her the potential for the growth you experienced from a small-company value fund.

How? We think you could do a lot worse than investing that $200,000 along the lines of Two Funds for Life, with the allocation based on her age.

If you have multiple heirs, you can set up accounts for each one. Or you could invest in a single fund, identify it in your will and specify how the proceeds should be divided.

Whatever you do along these lines for children or grandchildren, we suggest you give them each a copy of this book so they understand your intentions.

## Path Four: If you want to keep getting the benefit of small-company value stocks.

If you've benefitted from the addition of a small-company value fund and, as a result, are in good shape financially, you are probably glad you took on the additional risk.

If you are quite comfortable keeping some of your money invested in small-company value stocks, then a 10% stake could add more than 0.5% a year to your long-term return.

It's entirely possible that over a 25- to 30-year retirement, that difference could give a 20% to 30% boost to the total of your retirement distributions plus what you leave behind for your heirs.

## Path Five: If you are in your mid-70's and ready to accept more risk than you'll find in the bond-centric portfolio of your target date fund.

By the time you retire, a majority of your target date fund will be invested in bonds. In this case, you might be comfortable taking more risk.

You could then part ways with that fund and try something new. This may seem like heresy, but it has some merit.

This path is built on a combination of two large, tried-and-true mutual funds: Vanguard Wellington and Vanguard Wellesley.

Vanguard is the largest mutual fund company; it takes a generally conservative investment approach, and its fund expenses are among the lowest.

To evaluate this path, recall the returns from 2008, an awful year for many investors.

It was a year when the Standard & Poor's 500 Index lost 37%, and many investors lost more. Wellington and Wellesley weren't exempt from pain, of course.

But Wellington, which normally holds 40% of its portfolio in bonds, lost only 22.2%; Wellesley, which typically holds 60% of its portfolio in bonds, lost only 9.8%.

These two funds' longer-term results are favorable.

- Since its inception in 1929, **Wellington** has compounded at 8.1%. Through 2019, it had 71 up years, 19 down ones.
- Since its inception in 1970, **Wellesley** has compounded at 9.5%. Through 2019, it had 42 up years and seven down years.

As we write this, the most recent 10-year returns are 10% for Wellington and 7.9% for Wellesley.

If your portfolio is ample for your needs, you can consider investing in either of these funds. One approach that many investors seem to like is a 50-50 combination of Wellesley and Wellington.

That would allocate your portfolio about equally between stocks and bonds—a combination we think is suitable for many retirees, especially those who have more than enough to cover their basic cost of living.

## Path Six: If you're comfortable that you're set, you can turn back the clock and invest as if you were younger.

Let's say the year is 2050 and you've just retired comfortably with your money safely invested in a 2050 target date fund. The majority of that fund is invested in bonds.

You're confident that you have enough resources, and you'd like to take a bit more risk than your fund offers. You like the idea of a target date fund, and you want to stick to just one fund.

Guess what: You can pretend you're young again and transfer some or all of your money to a target date fund designed for younger investors. In this example, if you fully expect to live at least 20 more years, there's nothing to say you can't move your portfolio into a fund with a target date 20 years in the future.

That will repeat the glide path that presumably served you well for the past 20 years, and your investments will gradually become more conservative without any further action required on your part.

This could easily add 0.5% to your long-term return while keeping your level of risk under control.

Because there are multiple target date funds available, you can essentially dial in your preferred level of risk by choosing a fund with a target date as near—or far—into the future as you like.

Whichever path you choose, if you have successfully achieved financial independence, you have lots of choices open to you. And when you're retired, it doesn't get much better than that.

# Section Four

# SPECIAL CIRCUMSTANCES

▲

## 21.

# If Your 401(k) Lacks a Small-Company Value Option

*"The most difficult thing is the decision to act.*
*The rest is merely tenacity."*
Amelia Earhart

Not all retirement plans include a U.S. small-company value fund.

But virtually every one offers either a small-company blend fund (often just called "small-company") or a large-company value fund (sometimes just called "value").

The solution here is pretty straightforward: Pick a small-company fund or a value fund and follow the Two Funds for Life strategy from Chapter 17 as if you were using a small-company value fund.

Your returns will likely be a bit lower, but your risk level probably will be a bit lower as well (see below).

If you're in this situation, you may want to reread Chapters 7 and 8.

To refresh your memory regarding small-company stocks, as we wrote in Chapter 7, over all the 40-year periods from 1928 through 2019, small-company stocks returned an average of 13.8%. The very best 40-year period produced a return of 16.7%, the worst, 10.7%.

The S&P 500's *average* 40-year return was 11%—just barely above the *worst* 40 years for small-company stocks.

To refresh your memory regarding value stocks, in Chapter 8 we reported that over the past 92 years, value stocks had three times as many profitable calendar years as losing years. And the average 40-year return of large-company value stocks was 13.5%, compared with 11% for the S&P 500.

Each type of stock—large-company value stocks and small-company stocks—gave investors markedly better results than the Standard & Poor's 500 Index.

Assuming that you have a long-term investment outlook, here's a repeat of an interesting table from Chapter 15 that compares the worst periods of three types of stocks to the best period of the S&P 500.

## Table 21-1: Worst 40-year periods, 1970–2019

| Standard & Poor's 500 Index BEST | 12.2% |
|---|---|
| U.S. large-company value stocks WORST | 13.1% |
| U.S. small-company blend stocks WORST | 12.5 % |
| U.S. small-company value stocks WORST | 15.4% |

The chief takeaway is that in any 40-year period during those 50 years, investors were certain to do better in any of these three (large-company value, small-company blend, small-company value) than if they held their money in the S&P 500.

Which of these should you choose? Frankly, you're not likely to go wrong with any of them.

One possible way to decide: Compare the expense ratios of your plan's large-company value fund and its small-company fund, then choose whichever has lower expenses.

Also, consider the following:

In Chapter 17, we described our research showing how a Two Funds for Life strategy might have fared from 1970 through 2019.

Our hypothetical analysis based on hundreds of tested combinations of actual returns showed that the addition of a small-company value fund would have boosted the average 40-year return by 39% while increasing risk by only 11%

Based on the same assumptions we used there, here's a similar table showing the results if either a large-company value fund or a small-company blend fund were substituted for a small-company value fund.

**Table 21-2: Target date fund alone vs. Two Funds for Life formula using small-company blend or large-company value, 1970–2019**

| | Vanguard-like target-date fund | Two Funds for Life with small-company blend | Two Funds for Life with large-company value |
|---|---|---|---|
| **40-year growth of $1,000/year plus inflation** | $793,000 | $955,000 | $980,000 |
| **Worst-ever drawdown (risk)** | 46% | 48% | 52% |

The bottom line: In this simulation, applying the Two Funds for Life formula with a small-company blend fund increased the average return by 20.4% (compared with a target date fund alone) while making almost no change in the level of risk, measured by the worst drawdown.

Alternatively, using a large-company value fund boosted the average return by 23.6% while increasing the worst drawdown by 13%.

Here's our conclusion: Even if you don't have access to a small-company value fund, you can still expect very good results from using either a small-company blend fund or a large-company value fund.

Which one will do better? There's no way to know in advance. But just like the choice between two flavors of ice cream, you're likely to be happy either way.

Paul Merriman and Richard Buck

## 22.

# If you don't have a 401(k) or similar plan

*"The grim irony of investing is that we investors as a group not only don't get what we pay for, we get precisely what we don't pay for."*
John C. Bogle

Not every investor has access to a 401(k) or similar plan. But if you have taxable income from wages or salary or business income, you can put money into an IRA.

(You can also invest in an IRA if you want to add more to your savings after you have reached the maximum contribution into your 401(k)).

The annual IRA contribution limits (in 2020: $6,000 for people under 50 years old and $7,000 for those 50 and older) are not as high as those in employer retirement plans.

But if you sock away $6,000 a year for several decades and invest it well, you can build a sizable retirement nest egg. To loop back to an example from Chapter 1, if you do that starting when you're 30 and your investments grow at 8% a year, you will have a little more than $1 million by the time you're 65.

When you have an IRA, you can pick and choose virtually any mutual fund or exchange-traded fund.

To open an IRA, you'll need a brokerage account. Either Vanguard or Fidelity would be a good choice for the custodian. They both have a good selection of commission-free exchange-traded funds and index-based target date funds. Be careful to choose a target date fund that is based on index funds instead of actively managed funds.

Once you have found a target date fund with a year that matches your retirement plans, choose an exchange-traded fund to boost its performance in accordance with our Two Funds for Life recommendations.

Your best exchange-traded fund choice for small-company value at either Vanguard or Fidelity is SPDR S&P Small Cap Value (AVUV). Those letters, in this case, AVUV, make up what's called a "ticker symbol."

They represent a specific stock or exchange-traded fund for trading on a stock exchange.

For a large-company value exchange-traded fund, we recommend Invesco S&P 500 Pure Value (RPV); for a small-company blend exchange-traded fund, go with iShares Core S&P Small-Cap (IJR).

A full list of recommended "best in class" mutual funds and exchange-traded fund, updated every two years, is available online at paulmerriman.com.

# Roth or traditional?

As noted in Chapter 11, IRAs come in two flavors. You have to choose one or the other when you open your account. The difference is all about taxes.

Whether you have a Roth or traditional IRA, there are no taxes due on your investment income as it grows inside the account. In each case, you will pay a penalty for withdrawing money before you reach age 59½ unless you meet certain requirements.

The following is not tax advice, just a quick-and-dirty overview.

# Traditional

In a traditional IRA, your contribution is tax-deductible in the year that you make it. This makes that

# CommunityBloodCenter

Affiliate of the NCH Healthcare System

**1100 Immokalee Rd. Suite 100, Naples, FL 34110**
(Mailing address only, not a donation center)

**(239) 624-4120** • **givebloodcbc.org**

- **Check website for donation locations & maps**
- **You can give blood every 56 days**
- **Eat before giving blood**
- **Be well hydrated on donation day**
- **Photo ID is required**

NCH Community Blood Center is located on the NCH North Naples Hospital Campus near the Brookdale Entrance:
**1190 Health Park Blvd. Naples, FL 34110**

### Hours:
Mon., Thurs., & Fri: 8 am - 4 pm
Tues. 11 am - 7pm
Closed on Wed., Sat., & Sun.

THOMAS ORR
2860 HATTERAS WAY
NAPLES FL 34119

647
295
9964

# Share your
# holiday spirit
# GIVE BLOOD!

Community
Blood Center
What's Collected Here...Stays Here!

## Give The Gift of Life & Get a Special Gift!

## Holiday Blood Drive Schedule

**Sun. 12/26: 1 - 5 PM**
Outback Steakhouse 27230 Bay Landing Dr. Bonita Springs 34135
Give a Pint, Get a Bloomin' Onion Gift Card

**Mon. 12/27: 9:30 AM - 1:30 PM**
Texas Roadhouse 6815 Collier Blvd. Naples 34114
$10 Texas Roadhouse Gift Card

**Tues. 12/28: 11 AM - 3 PM**
Royal Scoop Homemade Ice Cream Berkshire Commons
7355 Radio Rd. Ste 104 Naples 34104
Give a Pint Get a Pint of Ice Cream

**Wed. 12/29: 11 AM - 3 PM**
Cruise Planners 834 Neapolitan Way Naples 34103
Gift Card from Community Blood Center & a Cruise Planner Reward Card
Valued at $100 Toward a Future Trip

**Thurs. 12/30: 10 AM - 2 PM**
Culvers Restaurant South Naples 5102 Tamiami Tr. E. Naples 34113
Give a Pint, Get a Pint of Culver's Custard & Culver's Gift Card

Community
Blood Center
Affiliate of the NCH Healthcare System

www.givebloodcbc.org
239.624.6505

**Photo ID & face masks are required on bloodmobile**

**No appointment is necessary**

contribution more affordable. However, later, when you withdraw from your IRA, everything you take out will be taxable income.

If you need the tax deduction in order to save, this may be the right option. The same is true if you are in a high tax bracket and believe you'll be in a lower bracket after you retire (although predicting future income tax rates is impossible).

When you reach age 72, you must begin withdrawing money from your IRA and paying taxes on the withdrawals. These "required minimum distributions" are determined by a formula that's known to all mutual fund companies and brokerages.

## Roth

In a Roth IRA, there's no tax deduction for your contribution. That's the bad news.

The good news comes when you take money out of the IRA in retirement: You won't owe taxes on any of it.

If you're trying to maximize your tax-sheltered savings, the Roth is the better choice. The Roth is also likely to give you more peace of mind when you retire, since you'll have tax-free withdrawals and no required distributions. If it suits your needs, you can leave the money in the account to grow tax-free.

Before you open any IRA account, either traditional IRA or Roth, make sure you are eligible, since the IRS limits the contributions and deductions for some high-income individuals.

Both types of IRA have other wrinkles that might or might not affect you. So before you open an account, consult with a tax advisor!

# Something else you can do in an IRA

As mentioned above, an IRA gives you seemingly unlimited choices of funds and exchange-traded funds.

If you're interested, you can take advantage of this to save some money (and thus boost your return) by creating a "do-it-yourself" target-date fund.

All that's necessary to replicate the equity investments in a typical target date fund is to invest 70% in a total U.S. market index fund and the rest in a total international market index fund. Fidelity offers those two funds with expense ratios of zero. That's right, zero.

Until you're 40 years old, your money should be mostly (if not entirely) in equities.

Therefore, until you reach 40, those two Fidelity funds could substitute for the target-date component of your Two Funds for Life strategy. The funds: Fidelity ZERO

Total Market Index Fund (FZROX) and Fidelity ZERO International Index Fund (FZILX).

To complement a target date fund, you'll still want to include a small-company value fund or exchange-traded fund to seek higher returns, and you'll pay expenses for that fund no matter how you handle the target date fund.

However, the benefits of this DIY alternative might be more than they appear at first.

The two Fidelity ZERO funds (available when Fidelity is your IRA custodian) cost nothing. A "index-based" target date fund is likely to charge around 0.15%. In addition, the unnecessary bonds in that fund will put a drag on your performance that will further reduce your return when compared with the two Fidelity funds.

How many actual dollars you'll save with this plan is hard to project, since it depends on the size of your account and your age (which determines the mix between the zero-expense Fidelity funds and your small-company value fund). Fidelity, by the way, has a very inexpensive small-company value fund with the ticker symbol FISVX.

However, every dollar you save in expenses is a dollar that belongs to you instead of Wall Street. And it's a dollar that can keep growing for you.

## 23.

# If You Don't Need a Glide Path

*"Save your money and someday your money will save you."*
Anonymous

What we're about to describe is indeed an unusual case, but we know someone who did this to put the lessons of Two Funds for Life to work.

He is responsible for investing some money for his family. The investment principal will not ever be needed. Instead, at the start of every year, the family withdraws 5% of the balance. The rest will be left to grow.

Each year, a designated group of family members will decide how to best use the 5% withdrawal to enhance the family's quality of life that year.

The investment goal is to have the principal grow over time despite these 5% annual withdrawals.

Our friend set this up with just two funds. The first is a relatively conservative base fund to provide reliable long-term growth with only moderate risk.

Since no "glide path" is needed for this portfolio, he chose Vanguard Wellington instead of a target date fund. Initially, 70% of the portfolio went into that fund, with the remaining 30% in a small-company value exchange-traded fund.

As mentioned in Chapter 20, Vanguard Wellington normally invests 60% of its assets in equities and 40% in bonds. This means this family portfolio started with 72% of its investments in equities, and 28% in bonds.

Our friend is comfortable with that allocation. The family's investment policy anticipates that over time, the small-company value fund will gradually make up a larger and larger portion of the whole portfolio.

Here's an interesting wrinkle: The two funds will not be rebalanced until and unless the small-company value fund grows so much that it makes up at least 50% of the total.

At that point, 80% of the portfolio would be invested in equities.

The funds would then be rebalanced, and the overall allocation would once again be 72% in equities.

Letting a small-company value fund grow and grow may seem pretty risky, but under this plan, the portfolio will always hold at least 20% in bonds.

This is a creative way to use a small-company value fund plus only one other fund for long-term growth.

Our friend could have specified an even higher starting percentage for small-company value (40% or even 50%) and let it grow to a higher limit (75% or 80%, for example).

He set it up the way he did in order to have the majority of the portfolio invested conservatively, in the Vanguard Wellington fund, and truly use small-company value only as a booster.

This whole arrangement is unusual, obviously, but it's an interesting variation on Two Funds for Life.

## 24.

# For Generous Parents or Grandparents: Investing for a Young Child

*"Compound interest is the eighth wonder of the world. He who understands it, earns it; he who doesn't, pays it."*

Attributed to Albert Einstein
(without evidence he actually said it)

If you're setting aside money for a young child, Two Funds for Life can work well with a few modifications.

The money for such a gift won't grow on a tree, but if you're a far-sighted and generous parent or grandparent, it could be easier than you think to give a young person a big head start.

This is especially true if you recall our advice in Chapter 2: Save earlier.

Consider this possibility: Sometime in a child's first year of life (ideally on the day they are born), you set aside $365. That's right, just $365, or $1 per day for that first year. Then keep up that savings rate every year until the child is old enough to take over this $1-a-day savings rate.

If you (and later the child) do this for 20 or 25 years, then this fortunate young adult will have a huge head start. The math is simple: 20 years of $1 a day comes to $7,300; add five more years, and there's $9,125. Invested at even a modest annualized rate of 10%, and the numbers are considerably larger: $20,912 after 20 years, $35,907 after 25.

From the start, this money should be invested in equities. We don't believe young investors are served well by investing in bonds before they are about 40, presumably 25 years from retirement.

However, many target date funds start with about 10% of their portfolios invested in bonds, even for the youngest investors. (The percentage of cash and bonds in Vanguard's 2065 fund in 2019, with 46 years to go, was 11%.)

As we saw in Chapter 13, a change in as little as 10% of a portfolio can make a huge long-term difference, and we see no reason that bonds should occupy even a little slice of a young person's portfolio.

Therefore, we think a Two Funds for Life investment for a young child should be an all-equity portfolio. The tricky question is how much of this young child's portfolio goes into a small-company value fund.

Though we believe strongly in small-company value, we think every investor needs at least some diversification. One good way to do that with two funds is to divide the portfolio equally between a small-company value fund and a large-company value fund.

This all-equity, all-value portfolio could be appropriate until age 35 or 40, at which time we'd suggest switching to the formula in Chapter 17. That would mean replacing the large-company value fund with a target date fund.

There really isn't any rocket science that will tell you exactly what combination will turn out the best.

To many people, the suggestion we just made will seem relatively aggressive. If you want the benefit of small-company value investing while holding only two funds in an overall package that's a bit more conservative, you could try this: Follow the Chapter 17 formula, using with the farthest-out Vanguard target date fund you can.

IRA accounts for minors may be hard to find, but Charles Schwab offers them, as well as mutual funds and exchange-traded funds suitable for following our recommendations.

Alternatively, you can open an account under the *Uniform Gifts to Minors Act*. However, when the beneficiary becomes an adult legally, they can use the assets in the account without restriction. This means you give up control.

If you want more control of the situation (and if you're willing to accept the tax consequences), you can open an account in your name and leave it in your will to the child.

In the meantime, as soon as the child has taxable earned income, they will be eligible to contribute to an IRA. At that point, you can withdraw enough from the account that you own and make the contribution into a Roth IRA. This way, you'll make sure the money goes to work tax-free inside the Roth IRA as soon as possible.

If you're contemplating anything like this, we suggest you have your plan reviewed ahead of time by a competent financial advisor who's familiar with tax laws.

Any way you do this, you'll be making a thoughtful, generous gift that could profoundly change somebody's life.

# Section Five

# BACK OF THE BOOK

▲

Paul Merriman and Richard Buck

# GLOSSARY

Here are definitions of some of the terms used in this book that may be unfamiliar.

A comprehensive glossary published by the U.S. government is available online at https://www.investor.gov/introduction-investing/investing-basics/glossary

Some of the following definitions are from that site, while we have adapted others to fit the terms as we use them in this book.

**Active management** — An attempt to exceed broad stock market returns through stock selection or through timing of purchases and sales, or both.

**Asset class** — Investments with similar characteristics. This is a common term used to identify things like stocks, bonds, cash, real estate and other investment vehicles. In this book, we're focused on different types of stocks, particularly small-company stocks and large-company stocks.

**Bear market** — A time when stock prices are declining and market sentiment is pessimistic. Generally, a bear market occurs when a broad market index falls by 20% or more over at least a two-month period.

**Blend fund** — A mutual fund that invests in both growth stocks and value stocks.

**Bond fund** — A mutual fund or exchange-traded fund that invests primarily in bonds and similar securities.

**Broker** — An individual who acts as an intermediary between a buyer and seller, usually charging a commission to execute trades.

**Bull market** — A time when stock prices are rising and market sentiment is optimistic. Generally, a bull market occurs when a broad market index rises by 20% or more over at least a two-month period.

**Capital gain** — The profit that comes when an investment is sold for more than the price the investor paid for it.

**Compound interest** — Interest paid on principal and on accumulated interest.

**Compound return** — A compound rate of return is the profit or loss on an investment over a one-year period, assuming the investment is not sold, expressed as a percentage. There are various ways of calculating this figure, which is sometimes referred to as a compound rate of return (CRR).

**Diversification/diversify** — A defensive investment strategy that can be neatly summed up as "Don't put all your eggs in one basket." In this book, diversification refers mostly to the practice of owning more than one asset class.

**Drawdown** — The difference in value of a portfolio between a high point and a subsequent lowest point, usually expressed as a percent of the high point.

**Exchange-traded fund (ETF)** — An investment company that's similar to a mutual fund except that it is traded on a stock exchange with a price that varies moment to moment, based on market prices, when the exchange is open for business.

**Expense ratio** — In a mutual fund or exchange-traded fund, the total annual operating expenses, including management fees, distribution fees, and other expenses, expressed as a percentage of average net assets.

**Glide path** — A plan of a mutual fund or portfolio to gradually change the level of risk over time by changing the overall mix of assets. In a target date fund, the glide path attempts to reduce overall risk as shareholders approach retirement.

**Growth stock or growth fund** — The stock of a company with a relatively high price-to-earnings ratio. A mutual fund that invests in such companies.

**Inflation** — A gradual increase in prices along with a decline in the purchasing power of money.

**Index fund** — A low-cost mutual fund designed to achieve approximately the same return as a stock index such as the Standard & Poor's 500 Index without attempting to buy or sell except when the components of the index change. Some index funds invest in all the companies included in an index; others invest in a representative sample.

**Large-company stocks** — Stocks with market capitalizations typically more than $10 billion, contrasting with small-company stocks, which typically average less than $3 billion.

**Load** — An upfront sales charge that investors pay when they buy mutual fund shares. The money is usually paid to compensate brokers. This charge reduces the amount of money that is actually invested for the benefit of the investor.

**Market capitalization** — The total value of a corporation determined by multiplying the current market price of one share of stock by the total number of outstanding shares. As used in this book, this term differentiates large-company stocks (large corporations) from small-company stocks.

**Market index** — A market index tracks the performance of a specific "basket" of stocks such as the

Standard & Poor's 500 Index or the Dow Jones Industrial Average.

**Mutual fund** — An investment company that continuously pools money from many investors and invests the money in stocks, bonds, money market instruments or other securities. Investors buy and sell shares in direct transactions with the fund or sometimes through a broker. Share prices are fixed at the end of each trading day, based on the prices of the assets in the fund's portfolio.

**Portfolio** — The combined investment holdings of an individual or a mutual fund.

**Price-to-earnings (P/E) ratio** — For a company with publicly traded stock, an indicator of whether the current stock price is high or low compared with past prices and/or compared with stock prices of other companies. The ratio is calculated by dividing the current stock price by the current earnings per share.

**Rebalancing** — A process, usually done once a year, designed to bring a portfolio back to its original and intended asset allocation. This is desirable because, over time, some investments grow faster than others, increasing or decreasing the portfolio's overall level of risk.

**Risk** — Investment risk is the possibility of losing money. Financial analysts often measure risk using a

statistic known as standard deviation, which gauges
the uncertainty of returns.

**Small-company stocks** — Stocks with market
capitalizations that typically average around $3 billion.
Contrasts with large-company stocks, which typically
average $50 billion.

**Target-date fund** — A diversified mutual fund that
uses a glide path to automatically shift toward a more
conservative mix of investments as it approaches a
target year when most of its investors will presumably
reach retirement age.

**Value stock or value fund** — The stock of a
company with a relatively low price-to-earnings ratio.
A mutual fund that invests in such companies.

# RESOURCES

This book is designed to give you the tools you'll need to turn a series of relatively modest investments into a lifetime of investing success. Our primary goal is to prod you into action, not to suggest a course of study.

Obviously there is a great deal more you can learn about investing. Once you have put Two Funds For Life into action, we believe you will benefit from reading and listening to some of the smartest people in the business.

The sources listed here are credible and reliable. However, some of them may be sponsored by advertisers who don't necessarily have your best financial interests in mind. So be careful in choosing where you put your trust.

## For young investors

If you have time for just one more book, you could do much worse than starting with *How to Think About Money* by Jonathan Clements. It's easy to read and packs a lifetime's worth of wisdom into fewer than 150 pages

If video is your preferred method of education, "2 Cents" on PBS is a terrific series. Topics in the first season included the lottery, the difficulty of saving for retirement, buying a house, the dumb financial decisions many people make, and whether the stock market is just a casino in disguise. https://www.pbs.org/show/two-cents/episodes/season/1/

**For investors interested in "retiring early"**

Choosefi.com offers a library of articles, podcasts and videos on what it takes to retire early. A good place to start is their beginners' guide.

At Fiology.com David Baughier offers a free 52-lesson online course and a free workbook.

**Financial planning education**

Thebalance.com has an extensive library of easy-to-read articles on lots of financial topics including investing and financial planning.

**More suggested reading**

You'll find an extensive library of articles on all aspects of investing at paulmerriman.com. There you'll also find free downloads of three "How to Invest" series books:

*First Time Investor: Grow and Protect Your Money*

*Get Smart or Get Screwed: How To Select The Best and Get The Most From Your Financial Advisor*

*101 Investment Decisions Guaranteed To Change Your Financial Future*

## Here are some of the best investment books we know:

*Your Money & Your Brain* by Jason Zweig

*The Little Book of Common Sense Investing* by John Bogle

*Personal Finance for Dummies* by Eric Tyson

*Investment Mistakes Even Smart Investors Make* by Larry Swedroe

*Think, Act and Invest like Warren Buffet* by Larry Swedroe
*Your Complete Guide to a Successful and Secure Retirement* by Larry Swedroe and Kevin Grogan

*Retire Before Mom and Dad* by Rob Berger

*The Little Book of Behavioral Investing* by James Montier

**Other books by Paul Merriman and Richard Buck**
Financial Fitness Forever — 5 Steps To More Money, Less Risk, More Peace of Mind

Live It Up Without Outliving Your Money: Creating The Perfect Retirement

# ABOUT THE AUTHORS

## Richard Buck

Richard Buck began subscribing to investment newsletters in high school, and he's never lost his fascination with all the ways money can be put to work. After college, he began a 30-year career as a journalist, including eight years as a writer and editor at The Associated Press and 20 years as a business reporter for *The Seattle Times*.

In 1993, he began writing for Paul Merriman; a few years later, he joined Paul's investment advisory firm as publications manager. He and Paul have worked together on countless articles and six other books, including *Financial Fitness Forever* and *Live It Up Without Outliving Your Money*. He has continued, since 2012, as Paul's trusted ghostwriter for The Merriman Financial Education Foundation.

Rich's writing has been published in travel magazines, outdoor magazines, electronics magazines, and in *America*, a publication of the U.S. State Department.

For retirement fun, he pursues a lifelong passion for radio by producing his own show, available online and at various stations nationwide. As his on-air persona,

Sam Waldron, Rich hosts "45 RPM, Music of the 40s and 50s", a musical journey back to the days when he was young. Each one-hour show combines stories and recordings centered on a theme.

In his spare time, he has been chairman of the board of a Seattle credit union, co-founder of a non-profit international exchange program, president of the Willamette University Alumni Association, and a member of the Willamette University Board of Trustees.

# Paul Merriman

Financial educator, author and podcaster, Paul is nationally recognized authority on mutual funds,index investing, asset allocation and both buy and-hold and active management strategies. He began his career in the 1960s, working briefly as a stock broker for a major Wall Street firm. Concluding that Wall Street was burdened with too many conflicts of interest, he decided to help small companies raise venture capital. In 1979, he became president and chairman of a public manufacturing company in the Pacific Northwest,
and in 1983 founded an investment advisory firm, Merriman Wealth Management (as it is now known). When he retired and sold the firm in 2012, it had $1.6 billion under management.

In 2011, Paul presented a Public Broadcasting Service special, "Financial Fitness Over 50", which was used as a fundraiser for PBS stations nationwide. This piqued his interest in teaching in retirement.

Upon retirement, he founded The Merriman Financial Education Foundation, a registered 501(c)(3) dedicated to providing free financial education to investors of all ages, especially do-it yourselfers, helping them make informed decisions and successfully implement their retirement savings strategy.

Through regular articles published on the Wall Street Journal's Marketwatch.com and free eBooks — co-authored with his long-time ghostwriter and friend Rich Buck — "Sound Investing" — an award-winning weekly podcast started in 1999 with Tom Cock and Don MacDonald — videos, newsletters, and recommendations for mutual fund and ETF portfolios, PaulMerriman.com has become a large and ever-growing resource of free original material to help investors of all ages.

In addition to the "How To Invest" series, Paul is author of four previous books on personal investing including, *Financial Fitness Forever: 5 Steps To More Money, Less Risk and More Peace of Mind* (McGraw Hill, Oct. 2011) and *Live It Up Without Outliving Your Money! Creating The Perfect Retirement*, (John Wiley & Sons, updated June 2008).

Since 2017, Paul has collaborated with Chris Pedersen and Daryl Bahls to create the 2 Funds for Life and 4-Fund Combo strategies, along with significant research on historical investment data.

A major Foundation project is the development and support of "Personal Investing," an accredited course at Paul's alma mater, Western Washington University.

Recipient of a distinguished alumni award from WWU's School of Economics, Paul is a founding and active member of the board of directors of Global HELP, a Seattle-based NPO providing medical publications free to doctors and health care workers in developing nations. A member of the Board of Directors of Bainbridge Community Foundation, he leads a series of financial workshops each spring.

Paul works for the Foundation without compensation. His return is the satisfaction from knowing he is helping individuals and their families build a more secure financial future. He lives on Bainbridge Island, Washington with his wife, Zan, two bichons and a chihuahua named Squish.

# ACKNOWLEDGEMENTS

## Paul & Rich

We are deeply grateful to the many people without whom this book would not have happened.

We're especially indebted to two key members of the Merriman Financial Education Foundation:

Chris Pedersen, director of research, suggested the basic structure of the strategy we have outlined here, and continued to guide us through the writing process.

Daryl Bahls, director of analytics, provided a wealth of data and scores of tables for our study in addition to those included in this book.

John Saul, Larry Swedroe and Susan Pelton gave us invaluable guidance and suggestions from the point of view of readers. Without their input, this book would not be nearly as good as it is.

Aysha Griffin, communications director, provided editorial consultation, proofread our manuscript and guided it into existence as a book. Margie Baxley, website manager, formatted the book into its present form. Jennifer Mah contributed strategies to increase sales to help support the foundation.

Our spouses, Zan Merriman and Susan Pelton, have given us unwavering support and encouragement.

In addition, each of us wants to recognize some people who made it possible for us as individuals to reach the starting point of this endeavor.

## From Rich

I'm grateful to the people who sparked my interest in money and investing and others who helped me mature as a writer.

To my grandfather, George Buck, who left a trust that helped me and my siblings pay for college and let us split what was left over. This made me realize I would someday have money to invest.

To the authors of a little book I bought when I was in college, who introduced me to fascinating concepts like international investing, dollar-cost averaging, and mutual funds.

Some people helped me realize I could be a writer.

To my 6th grade teacher, Mrs. Edwards, the first person I ever remember remarking (to the whole class, no less) that I was a good writer.

To Stan Youngs, who responded to a letter I wrote him in my early teens by writing back to say he was impressed by how I had written it.

To my college astronomy professor, Maurice Stewart, who announced to our class that a paper I had written was excellent and had taught him some things. (Wow!) He said he gave the paper a grade of "C." When I asked in astonishment why, he replied: "You made two grammatical errors. Those seem unimportant, I know. They are so unimportant that there is no excuse for them."

To three editors after college:

- Frank Gayman, city editor of the Yakima Herald, who taught me to fear vague and sloppy writing. One day, Frank read about half a story I had given him. Then while everybody in the newsroom could see, Frank (we typed our stories on paper back then) tossed my work on the floor and bellowed: "Buck! Write this in English!"
- Basil Raffety, the editor at the first Associated Press bureau where I worked, who taught me to trust my instincts.
- Steve Dunphy, business editor at The Seattle Times, who gave me license to be creative and showed by example how to make financial writing meaningful to non-financial people.

I'm also grateful to many other people who tolerated my shortcomings (of which there were plenty) and celebrated my successes over the years.

## From Paul

I'm deeply grateful to all the people who taught me about investing over the past half-century. First and foremost, the thousands of investors who trusted me to help them through the unending string of ups and downs in the market. They taught me by example what worked and (in a few memorable cases) what didn't work. They shared their hopes, their fears, their successes and their frustrations.

Many of these people became my friends, and I learned more from them than I can ever repay.

I learned still more from my colleagues over 30 years while building an advisory firm that operated under several names and is now known as Merriman Wealth Management. These dedicated professionals put up with my singing, my faulty memory, and my messy office. Their talents and knowledge opened my eyes to parts of the investment world I could have otherwise missed.

I was blessed to have my son, Jeff, working hand-in-hand with me as we built the firm.

I'm especially indebted to my personal Merriman advisor, Tyler Bartlett. Among his many services, Tyler keeps me on track by insulating my investments from my emotions.

Thanks to the people who, after I retired at age 69, introduced me to new opportunities, including a national PBS TV presentation, a regular column (still going) at MarketWatch.com, plus countless speaking engagements and lots of media exposure.

I've learned a lot from some of the best brains in the business, including Warren Buffett, Larry Swedroe, Mark Hulbert, and the late John Bogle.

My wife, Zan Merriman, encouraged me to focus my retirement on helping first-time investors. That led to the creation of The Merriman Financial Education Foundation, a continuing financial education project at Western Washington University, years of producing podcasts, articles, videos and other educational materials, and to this book. Zan has accepted a very different retirement life than she had imagined; being married to a workaholic is not easy, but her support has never failed me.

Made in United States
North Haven, CT
18 December 2021

13228963R00104